Haydn: his life and times

HAYDN

his life and times

Neil Butterworth

MIDAS BOOKS

By the same author
A Music Quiz (Foreword by Joseph Cooper)
In the same illustrated documentary series
General Editor: Ateş Orga
CHOPIN   Ateş Orga
MOZART   Peggy Woodford
MENDELSSOHN   Ateş Orga (in preparation)
SCHUBERT   Peggy Woodford (in preparation)

First published in 1977 by
Midas Books
12 Dene Way, Speldhurst, Tunbridge Wells, Kent TN3 0NX

© Neil Butterworth 1977
by arrangement with International Authors Agency

ISBN 0   85936   070   9

Printed in Great Britain by
Chapel River Press, Andover, Hants.

Contents

Acknowledgements

The Editor and Publishers would like to thank the following for kindly granting reproduction rights:

Her Majesty Queen Elizabeth II

Beethoven-Haus, Bonn
British Museum, London
Gesellschaft der Musikfreunde, Vienna
Kunsthistorisches Museum, Vienna
Library of Congress, Washington
Metropolitan Museum of Art, New York
Monastery of St. Florian
Nationalbibliothek, Vienna
National Portrait Gallery, London
Öffentliche Wissenschaftliche Bibliothek, Berlin
Royal College of Music, London
Royal Swedish Musical Academy, Stockholm
Universitätsbibliothek, Tübingen
Vatican Art Gallery, Rome

Wadhurst, January, 1977   *A.O.*

Bibliography

Anderson, Emily *Letters of Beethoven*, 3 vols. (London 1961)

Anderson, Emily *Letters of Mozart and his Family*, 2 vols., rev. (London 1966)

Carpani, G. *Le Haydine* (Milan 1812)

Dies, A. C. *Biographische Nachrichten über Joseph Haydn* (Vienna 1810)

Gal, Hans *The Golden Age of Vienna* (London 1948)

Geiringer, Karl *Haydn: a Creative Life in Music* (New York 1946, rev. ed. 1963)

Griesenger, G. A. *Biographische Notizen über Joseph Haydn* (Leipzig 1810)

Hoboken, Anthony van *Joseph Haydn: Thematisch-bibliographisches Werkverzeichnis*, Vol. I (Mainz & London 1957)

Hughes, Rosemary *Haydn* (London 1950)

Landon, H. C. Robbins *Collected Correspondence and London Notebooks of Joseph Haydn* (London 1959)

— *Essays on the Viennese Classical Style* (London 1970)

— *The Symphonies of Joseph Haydn* (London 1955)

Pohl, C. F. 'Haydn', *Grove's Dictionary of Music and Musicians*, Vol. IV (London 1954)

Rochlitz, J. F. *Für Freunde der Tonkunst* (Leipzig 1824-1832)

Scott, Marion M. 'Catalogue of Haydn's Works', *Grove's Dictionary of Music and Musicians*, Vol. IV (London 1954)

Frontispiece (*and cover*) Haydn. Portrait in oils by Thomas Hardy, 1791 (London, Royal College of Music)

Chapter 1

Beginnings

'The genius of common sense'—Hans Gal

Franz Joseph Haydn was born in 1732 in the small town of Rohrau in Eastern Austria near the border with Hungary. Although the family register gives the actual date of birth as 1 April, Haydn himself said that he was born on the night of 31 March. In a short biographical study published in 1778, however, he is also reported to have stated: 'My brother Michael preferred to claim that I was born on 31 March because he did not want people to say I had come into the world as an April fool.'*

Haydn's birthplace. An early engraving

His father, Mathias Haydn, was a master wheelwright who married Maria Koller in 1728 and settled in the town of Rohrau. Although Mathias could not read music, he had acquired a harp which he learnt to play while travelling through Germany and Austria as a journeyman wheelwright soon after completing his apprenticeship. This appears to be the sole source of the young

* A friend of the composer, J. C. Rosenbaum, categorically wrote in his *Diary* (Vienna National Library) that the birth took place at 4.0 pm on the afternoon of 31 March.

9

Joseph's musical inheritance. Mathias enjoyed playing the harp accompaniment to his own singing of Austrian folk-songs. Although he seems to have lived a simple life, he was much respected by the townspeople and rose to become a local official responsible to his patron, Count Harrach, for the good conduct of the citizens and for the maintenance of local amenities such as the condition of the roads.

Haydn inherited his father's administrative efficiency as can be seen in the thoroughly competent way he managed the musical affairs at Eisenstadt and Esterháza where he had sole charge of every aspect of musical life including the well-being of the musicians under him.

The town of Rohrau lies in a marshy district which even today is hardly an attractive place. The house in which Haydn was born is still standing. Mathias had twelve children but six of them died in infancy. The survivors were Francesca (1730–1781), Joseph (1732–1809), Anna Maria (d. 1802), Anna Katharina, Johann Evangelist (d. 1805), and Johann Michael (1737–1806).

Haydn's birthplace today. A photograph

The young Joseph, nicknamed *Sepperl* by the family, revealed a remarkable musical talent at an early age. He possessed a fine singing voice and showed a strong desire to learn the violin which he had seen played by the local schoolmaster. Musical opportunities in such a small community as Rohrau were naturally very limited for a boy of obvious gifts. When Joseph was five years old, the Haydn family were visited by a cousin of Mathias who lived in Hainburg, a town a few miles from Rohrau. This man, Johann Mathias Franck, was a schoolmaster and precentor at the local church where he was responsible for the music. It was he who suggested to Mathias that *Sepperl* should return with him to

Charles VI (1685–1740), Emperor of Austria, King of Bohemia, and King of Hungary. A noted patron of learning and the arts, he was particularly fond of music. A contemporary painting (Vienna, Nationalbibliothek)

Hainburg where the boy could receive a far better musical education than could be provided in Rohrau. Although Haydn's mother had initial misgivings over parting with her boy who was still only five years old, Haydn eventually went to Hainburg, probably at the age of six. Thereafter he was not to return to his home town, except for brief visits.

One can imagine the considerable change which took place in the child's mind. Life in Hainburg was full of activity compared to the monotony of Rohrau. Although he may have felt homesick at times, little Joseph was now fully occupied with a daily routine which seems by today's standards to be particularly severe for one so young. From 7.0 am to 10.0 am there were school lessons, followed by Mass in the church. After the midday meal, the boys of the school worked at their lessons again from noon until 3.0 pm. When this arduous day was over, Haydn and his companions received instruction in the violin and clavier. Haydn's early biographer, Albert Christoph Dies, tells how the six-year old boy also learnt to play the drum in a Holy Week procession, to replace Franck's drummer who had recently died. The drum was tied onto the back of a hunchback so that the little boy could play it. The drum is still preserved in the church at Hainburg.

During his two years with Franck, Haydn acquired a remarkable knowledge of music through taking part in all the musical events of the town. His stay was rigorous but in other ways most rewarding. At the end of his life, Haydn paid tribute to his teacher: 'I shall be grateful to that man as long as I live for keeping me so hard at work.' The only feature of the Hainburg household which distressed him was that the high standard of cleanliness which his mother had instilled into him was ignored by Franck's wife, so that the boy's clothes were seldom washed or repaired.

I could not help perceiving, much to my distress that I was gradually getting very dirty, and though I thought a good deal of my little person, was not always able to avoid spots of dirt on my clothes, of which I was dreadfully ashamed; in fact I was a regular little urchin.

In 1738 Mathias Haydn made a trip to Hainburg to attend a ceremony to bond a new apprentice wheelwright. No doubt the boy was very pleased to see his father on this occasion.

In 1740 Karl Georg Reutter, the newly appointed choirmaster at St. Stephen's Cathedral in Vienna, visited Hainburg in search of new choristers. Through the pastor of the town he heard of the talented young Haydn.

Reutter was much impressed by his singing and agreed to take the boy into his choir when he had reached the age of eight. Mathias and Maria Haydn were delighted at the opportunity

Der Stock am Eisen Platz.   *La Place dit Stock am Eisen*

The centre of Vienna as it must have looked to the young Haydn. St. Stephen's is in the background. Coloured engraving by Karl Schütz, 1779

given to their son to further his education. Before the move to Vienna, Haydn improved his vocal technique on his own as Franck was apparently unable to teach him exercises to develop his voice.

Little *Sepperl's* transfer from the backwoods of Rohrau to Hainburg must have been a notable change of environment, but the thought of going from this small provincial town to the capital city itself fired the imagination of the child who became impatient to see for himself the marvels of Vienna, especially the famous cathedral which was to become his home for the next nine years.

Chapter 2

Vienna—the early years

'The mind and soul must be free'—Haydn

The splendour of Vienna was at its height in the 1740s when Haydn became a choir boy in the Cathedral of St. Stephen. The huge buildings, palaces, churches and the cathedral itself must have created a very strong awe-inspiring impression upon the child.

Karl Georg Reutter, the *Kapellmeister*, or musical director at St. Stephen's, was born in Vienna in 1708, the son of a previous *Kapellmeister* at the cathedral. He was the composer of a large quantity of church music, including nine oratorios, and wrote thirty-one operas while acting as composer at the Austrian court, a position he obtained in 1731 at the age of only twenty-three. Reutter appears to have been a man of considerable personal ambition, acquiring one important musical post in Vienna after another, which left him little time to concentrate on the welfare and instruction of the choristers in his charge. As a composer he was very popular in Vienna during his lifetime, but little of his music has survived to the present day.

If the daily routine in Franck's Hainburg choir school seems rigorous to us today, life in St. Stephen's must be reckoned even more severe. The cathedral authorities paid Reutter 700 gulden a year for the board and education of each chorister. Although this sum of money was perhaps inadequate, Reutter neglected his charges who were very poorly fed. As a result, the boys looked forward eagerly to every occasion when the choir sang at functions outside the cathedral duties. At such times they were treated to fine feeds, so that like his companions, Haydn contrived to be invited as a member of every visiting group of singers, since this was the only means whereby he could obtain a decent meal.

Reutter's disregard of the well-being of the boys extended to their education, as well as their stomachs. The old-fashioned educational practices stipulated that religious instruction, Latin, mathematics and writing were the only important subjects. The musical side included tuition in singing, violin and clavier, but there was no instruction in theory or composition. Naturally, church services occupied much of the time of these small boys so that opportunities for music lessons and practising were very limited. Not surprisingly, Reutter's only interest in teaching music to his choristers was to improve their performances in the cathedral. Although he discovered Haydn one day trying to write a *Salve Regina* for twelve voices, he was too busy to offer advice or help to the aspiring composer. Haydn later stated that he received only two lessons in theory from the *Kapellmeister* during the whole of his time in the choir.

Nevertheless the eager boy studied very carefully the music he had to sing in the church services and thereby acquired a practical knowledge of musical technique from the works of Caldara, Fux and Reutter himself. According to Johann Friedrich Rochlitz (1832), Haydn claimed that he

Vienna. Engraving, anonymous, early 18th century

. . . never had a proper teacher. I started with the practical side, first in singing, then in playing instruments and later in composition. I listened more than I studied. I listened attentively and tried to turn to good account what most impressed me. In this way my knowledge and ability were developed. I heard the finest music in all forms that

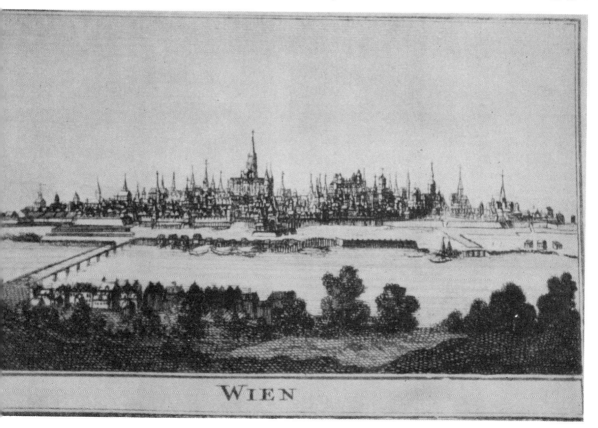

WIEN

15

was to be heard in my time, and of that there was much in Vienna.

The educational system was conducted in part on a monitorial basis, so that the older boys taught the younger ones. In this way Joseph acted as the teacher of his brother, Michael, who joined the choir a few years later. His other brother, Johann Evangelist, also became one of the cathedral choristers.

In spite of the privations of daily life, Haydn enjoyed much of his stay in Vienna. He was impressed by the elaborate ceremonies and processions connected with the religious festivities at the cathedral. The choristers often took part in open-air pageants and other activities which greatly excited the imagination of the young boy. On one visit of the choir to the palace of Schönbrunn in Vienna, which the Empress Maria Theresia had recently had

The Schönbrunn Palace in the 18th century. Painting by Bernardo Bellotto (Vienna, Kunsthistorisches Museum)

constructed, some of the boys climbed the scaffolding which was still round the walls. This aroused the displeasure of the Empress herself who threatened them with a whipping if they were seen there again. The following day Joseph was unable to resist the temptation and was duly punished for his audacity.

As was to be expected, Haydn's voice began to deteriorate as he reached his mid-teens. He tried hard to disguise this, but when the Empress complained of his dreadful singing, it was clear that his time in the choir was soon to end. Furthermore, the young Michael Haydn was receiving adulations in regard to his excellent singing voice. Although he made no comments, the rising success of his brother must have created a natural jealousy in the older boy who was soon to be expelled. One can see that it would require the qualities of a saint for him not to have felt depressed

16

as Michael took over the solo singing parts hitherto performed by Joseph.

His actual departure from the cathedral came suddenly, although he must have been expecting dismissal at any time. As a foolish prank, he cut off the pigtail of a fellow chorister. When Reutter threatened to cane him, Haydn said that he would rather leave the choir than submit to the punishment. Reutter, perhaps glad to have the excuse, promptly expelled the boy, but only after he had caned him.

So on a cold November morning in 1749, the seventeen-year old Haydn found himself in the streets of Vienna, without money or lodgings and totally unprepared to earn a living for himself.

Maria Theresia (1717–80), daughter of Charles VI, Empress of Austria, Queen of Bohemia and Hungary, consort of Franz I—with her family. Painting by Martin van Meytens, *c.* 1752 (Vienna, Nationalbibliothek)

Vienna, a view of the
city from the Joseph-
stadt. Coloured
engraving by Schütz,
1785

Chapter 3

Growing up

'What I am is all the result of the direst need'—Haydn

It was fortunate that on the day following his dismissal, the destitute Haydn met Johann Michael Spangler, a singer in another church in Vienna, with whom he was slightly acquainted. Although Spangler himself was poor, and had a wife and child to keep, he invited Haydn to share his small garret lodging. In this way, Haydn at least had shelter for the winter, but hardly any likelihood of earning any money. On his own admission, he was not a good enough violinist to find a post in any court orchestra, and his singing voice had ceased to be of any use to him. In addition, the inadequate education he had received under Reutter prepared him for no suitable occupation even outside music. Haydn's mother had at one time hoped her son would become a priest, but he did not seem seriously to have considered going into the Church as a solution to his predicament.

For a few months Haydn stayed with the Spanglers, earning a little money by composing and arranging instrumental music, playing in out-door serenades and giving music lessons. Early the following year, he left Vienna as the Spanglers were expecting another baby and there would be no room for a lodger in such a tiny garret.

He made a pilgrimage to the shrine of the Virgin of Mariazell in Styria. Here he hoped to obtain a post in the chapel choir where the choirmaster, Florian Wrastil, was a former singer at St. Stephen's. At first Haydn was turned away, but his persistence was rewarded when he crept into the church and took up a copy of the music the choir was singing and sight-read perfectly the difficult solo. As a result he stayed there a week, singing in the choir, but more important, he received proper meals for the first time in months. The singers at Mariazell also made a small collection for the poor young man who returned to Vienna in somewhat higher spirits than he had left.

In Vienna he received another stroke of good fortune. A colleague of Mathias Haydn, Anton Buchholz, lent the aspiring

Vienna, the 'New Market'. In the background is the Schwarzenberg Palace where Haydn's last works were to be performed. On the left is the 'Mehlgrube', the first floor rooms of which were mainly used for dancing. Coloured engraving by Schütz

Vienna, the old
Michaelerhaus

composer the sum of 150 florins, free of interest or a date for
repayment. With this apparent fortune, Haydn was able to rent
his own room at the top of a house in the Michaelerhaus, a
district of Vienna near the Kohlmarkt and the Church of St.
Michael where Spangler was a singer. Here he set to work to
study musical theory in great earnestness. He bought a copy of
Gradus ad Parnassum by Fux and another treatise by Johann

Carl Philipp Emanuel
Bach (1714–88). Pastel
by Johann Philipp
Bach, 1773 (Paul Bach
Collection, Eisenach)

Matheson. It was at this time, too, that he discovered the first six keyboard sonatas (the *Prussian* set of 1742) by C. P. E. Bach, the son of the now more famous Johann Sebastian Bach. These works made a considerable impression upon Haydn. He told Dies: 'I did not leave the clavier until I could play them all. I played them especially when I was depressed and always left the instrument in good spirits.' Haydn's earliest surviving composition, a *Missa Brevis* in F is one of the works written during this period of his life.

In 1752 Haydn composed the music for a burlesque opera called *Der Krumme Teufel* (*The Lame Devil*). This achieved a

The Imperial Court
Poet, Pietro Metastasio
(1698–1782)

Aloysia Weber (1760–
1839), Mozart's first
great love

considerable but brief success, as a Viennese nobleman thought that the main character was a caricature of himself and the opera was banned from performance.

Another piece of good fortune for Haydn was that in the house in which he lodged lived the famous Italian poet and librettist Metastasio who had provided texts for most of the important composers of opera including Handel, Gluck and Caldara. In 1754, through this man, Haydn acquired a promising piano pupil, Marianne Martinez, the ten-year old daughter of a Spanish nobleman who also lived in the Michaelerhaus apartment. Every day for three years Haydn taught this girl, receiving in return free board.

Marianne later became a leading musical figure in Vienna, talented equally as a singer, pianist and composer. She once played keyboard duets with Mozart. It was through Marianne that Haydn came into contact with the famous Italian singing teacher and composer, Niccolò Porpora. Marianne was receiving singing lessons from Porpora and Haydn became her accompanist at these classes.

Haydn learnt much from Porpora, a man then 'sour beyond all that can be imagined', by closely observing his teaching methods. He acted as musician valet to the old man, who even took him on a number of visits. The most important of these was to the summer spa at Mannersdorf in Hungary where Haydn met Gluck. Porpora offered valuable criticism of Haydn's compositions and helped his pupil-servant to improve his Italian.

Also in 1754, Haydn received the news of his mother's death at the age of forty-seven. His father, then aged fifty-five, soon afterwards married his servant girl who was only nineteen years old. Thus Haydn acquired a step-mother who was three years his junior.

Gradually Haydn was making himself known in the musical circles of Vienna, but he himself said: 'I had to eke out a wretched existence for eight years.' Through one of his aristocratic pupils, Countess Thun, he obtained entrance to the upper class musical society. At one of these chamber music evenings he made the acquaintance of Karl Joseph von Fürnberg who engaged him as a violinist at his country house outside Vienna. It was for these occasions that Haydn composed his first string quartets. From these performances he suddenly found himself widely known and in great demand as an instrumentalist and teacher, so that although he worked hard from morning until night, for the first time in his life he was earning a satisfactory living.

In 1758 Haydn obtained his first permanent musical post. Fürnberg recommended him to Count Ferdinand Maximilian von

Vienna, 'Am Hof'. On the left is the Collalto Palace where the young Mozart and his sister first played for the Viennese nobility in 1762

Morzin, an ardent music lover. The annual salary was 200 florins, not a fortune, but enough to ensure the composer some security.

It was for the orchestra he now directed that Haydn wrote his first orchestral pieces. At the Morzin summer residence at Lukaveč (in present-day Czechoslovakia) Haydn's First Symphony was performed one evening, with the composer directing from the harpsichord in the traditional manner of the period. It was a distinct success with the aristocratic audience to whom it was played. One of those present, Prince Anton Esterházy, was to become an important person in Haydn's life.

Now that he had acquired secure employment, Haydn felt that he was in a position to get married. Although we know little of his personal life at this time, it is certain that he fell in love with one of his pupils, Therese Keller, the younger daughter of a Viennese hairdresser. Her brother had been a violinist at St. Stephen's when Haydn was a chorister there. Apparently she did

not return his affection, and in 1756 she entered the convent of
St. Nicholas in Vienna. For her induction ceremony, Haydn
composed an Organ Concerto in C and probably the *Salve
Regina* in E for two sopranos, chorus and organ, a work showing
the influence of his teacher, Porpora.

For reasons that are quite unknown, Haydn married Therese's
sister Maria Anna. Perhaps he had become so closely associated
with the family that he felt a curious moral obligation to marry
the other daughter. It is also possible that pressure was brought
to bear upon him in some way. It is extremely unlikely that he
lacked interest in the opposite sex and married merely for the sake
of convention since he later developed very close friendships with
a number of women. Whatever prompted him to marry Maria
Anna we shall never know, but the result proved to be a serious
miscalculation on his part. The marriage took place on 26 November 1760 in St. Stephen's. The fact that she was three years older

26

than Haydn and not particularly good looking need not have been insurmountable obstacles to a happy marriage, but it was soon evident to the composer that she was ill-natured, totally indifferent to music and quite incapable of providing either a home or children.

Subsequent domestic life must have been painful to both parties, since they constantly quarrelled over even petty matters. According to the musicians who worked under Haydn, Maria Anna was constantly indulging in actions designed to irritate her husband. It is said that she used his manuscripts as lining to her pastry tins and as hair curlers. However it is perhaps unfair to place all the blame upon her for the failure of the marriage. As an escape, Haydn turned to his music to avoid the turbulent life at home, and his wife devoted much of her time to the church.

It is interesting to note the parallel with the life of Mozart. He, too, fell in love with a girl who would not marry him and he married instead her younger sister. Aloysia Weber's reason for rejecting the young Mozart is clearly that he had no financial security as he had recently been dismissed by the Archbishop of Salzburg. She married the artist and actor, Josef Lange. Constanze Weber was not the shrewish wife that Maria Anna soon became, but her management of domestic affairs was chaotic and extravagant. Nevertheless Mozart's married life was no doubt a happy one in spite of the numerous problems which arose as a result of Constanze's poor health.

Early in 1761, Count Morzin was forced to disband his orchestra through financial difficulties so that Haydn had to look for another post. Prince Paul Anton Esterházy heard that Haydn was unemployed and at once offered him the appointment of assistant conductor of his orchestra at Eisenstadt, his palace near Vienna.

The Esterházy Palace at Eisenstadt. Coloured steel engraving by C. Rohrich after L. Rohbock

27

Chapter 4

The Esterházys and Eisenstadt

'My prince was always satisfied with my works'—Haydn

Since the Hungarian War of Independence under Rákóczi had been put down in 1711, the Austrian Court had deliberately strengthened the position of the Hungarian aristocracy in order to keep them loyal to the Austro-Hungarian Empire and to maintain an indirect control over the Hungarian people to prevent any further popular risings.

The foremost family in Hungary in the eighteenth century was the House of Esterházy of Galanta. Its beginning is traced back to the early seventeenth century when Nicholas (Miklos) Esterházy, born in 1583, was expelled from his Protestant family for espousing the Catholic faith. He twice married young rich widows and thereby amassed a considerable fortune. His strong support for the Catholic cause made him leader of the Habsburg party and in 1625 he was elected Palatine of Hungary.

Through various political and religious intrigues, Nicholas became the possessor of numerous estates including that of Eisenstadt which he was given as compensation for ceding other lands to Gabor Bethlen, Prince of Transylvania. On his death, he was succeeded first by his eldest son Laszlo and shortly afterwards in 1652 by his other son, Paul. Like Nicholas, Paul married twice, each time acquiring enormous wealth and property. On his death the Esterházy family owned twenty-five castles and palaces and about one and a half million acres of land. It was Paul who in 1683 built the magnificent castle at Eisenstadt.

Paul Anton Esterházy inherited the title of Palatine at the age of ten on the death of Prince Joseph Esterházy in 1720, but he did not begin his reign until he came of age in 1734 when he was twenty-four. He initiated extensive improvements to the palace at Eisenstadt, and the gardens were remodelled on the French style.

He also founded the permanent orchestra with Gregor Werner (1695–1766) as musical director and Luigi Tommasini (1741–1808) as eventual leader. He also established a library of opera scores and libretti which he collected from throughout Germany and Italy: these have been preserved in the National Library in Budapest. The detailed catalogues of this collection compiled in 1756 and 1759 were destroyed in the liberation of Budapest in 1945.

Prince Paul Anton also took a great interest in the theatre and arranged for dramatic performances and operas to be given regularly at Eisenstadt. Most of the actors and opera singers were from visiting companies although they usually stayed for a long season often lasting many months.

When Haydn entered the service of the Esterházy household, the orchestra, choir and company of actors were established features of everyday life at Eisenstadt.

The contract which was drawn up for the employment of Haydn by the Prince is still extant. By present day standards, the terms seem very restrictive and severe in several of the conditions, but in the eighteenth century, these would have been accepted as the normal regulations applicable to a servant in Haydn's position.

The contract safeguarded the position of the aged Werner, but Haydn was given sole control of the orchestra. He was also promised the post of *Kapellmeister* upon Werner's retirement or

The Bergkirche in Eisenstadt. Lithograph by A. L. Jung after a drawing by Michael Mayer, 1840. It was here that Beethoven's Mass in C, commissioned by Prince Nicholas Esterházy II, was first performed in 1807, less than two years before Haydn's death

31

death, provided that he had discharged his duties to the satisfaction of the Prince. He was also to conduct himself soberly and set an example to the other musicians who were placed in his charge. Any minor disputes among the players were to be settled by him.

Every day the composer had to present himself in livery before the Prince at midday to receive instructions regarding the music to be played. All the compositions he wrote were to be for the exclusive use of the Prince; although the clause forbade the writing or copying of Haydn's music for performance outside Eisenstadt, this was either ignored or annulled later, although, to begin with, Haydn certainly devoted almost all his energies to the music used at the castle.

He also had to train the singers, maintain his own proficiency as a performer and see to the maintenance of the musical instruments. The contract, signed in Vienna on 1 May 1761, was to remain in force for three years, although Haydn could be dismissed at any time if found negligent. On the other hand, he was required to give six months' notice if he wished to leave. The annual salary was fixed at 400 florins, twice the amount he had received from Count Morzin.

Although Haydn was a servant under an autocratic, almost feudal, system he enjoyed a position whereby he could write almost any music he pleased and hear it in performance.

My Prince was always satisfied with my works: I not only had the encouragement of constant approval but as conductor of the orchestra, I could make experiments, observe what produced an effect and what weakened it, and was thus in a position to improve, alter and make additions or omissions, and be as bold as I pleased. I was cut off from the world, there was no-one to confuse or torment me and I was forced to become original.

Shortly after his arrival at Eisenstadt, the orchestra was augmented to consist of five violins or violas, one cello, one double bass, one flute, two oboes, two bassoons, two horns and one pensioned timpani player (according to Pohl). The choir was even smaller: two sopranos, one alto, two tenors and one bass. The wind players also constituted the military band.

The first works that Haydn wrote for the Prince were three symphonies: No. 6 in D *Le Matin*, No. 7 in C *Le Midi*, and No. 8 in G *Le Soir*. These titles were suggested by the Prince himself and the names imply some kind of programmatic basis. The use of *concertante* solo parts especially for the violin and cello hark back to the *concerto grosso* of the Italian school of composers and of Handel who had died only two years earlier in London. These

Prince Nicholas
Esterházy I, Haydn's
patron. After a portrait
by J. L. Tocque, 1758

symphonies maintain a brilliant gaiety throughout to impress the company and to arouse the admiration and gratitude of the orchestra who no doubt much enjoyed this youthful spirited music.

Prince Paul Anton was a keen music lover and a performer on both the violin and the cello. His enthusiasm for opera is reflected in the collection of scores and libretti and Haydn seemed very satisfied to serve under him.

On 18 March 1762, less than a year after Haydn's appointment, Prince Paul Anton Esterházy died.

Prince Nicholas (Miklos), Paul Anton's brother and successor, was given the epithet 'Magnificent' for his delight in extravagant entertainments and the grandeur with which he endowed his surroundings. Like Paul Anton, he possessed a genuine interest in music and played the baryton (viola di bordone), an instrument now obsolete which belonged to the *viol da gamba* family. It had six gut strings on the front and a number of metal strings attached to the neck of the instrument at the back which acted as sympathetic resonators to the bowed notes, but could also be plucked simultaneously with the left hand while the player bowed on the other side.

Because of the difficulties presented to the performer, this instrument achieved only a limited popularity, but unfortunately for Haydn, the Prince was an avid enthusiast. For this reason he had to provide his master with music specially written for him. Between 1762 and 1775 he composed about 160 divertimenti for baryton, viola and cello, of which 126 have survived. Haydn himself learnt to play the baryton, thereby incurring the displeasure of the Prince who viewed the composer as a rival who might damage his own pride and prestige as a performer on the unique instrument.

Prince Nicholas Esterházy, now aged 49, was installed as the new prince at a magnificent ceremony on 17 May 1762 at Eisenstadt. The celebrations ordered for this important event included four short operas by Haydn which were the first of his compositions for the stage at Eisenstadt.

The only music from these to have survived is now in the National Library in Budapest and comprises of *La Marchesa di Nespoli* (*The Marchioness of Nespoli*), based on the Italian Commedia dell' Arte characters of Columbine, Pantallon and Sganarello. The other three were probably short scenes or intermezzi to be performed as light relief between the acts of a larger and more serious work. They are *La vedova* (*The Widow*), *Il dottore* (*The Doctor*) and *Il Sganarello*.

For the wedding of his son Anton (Antal) to the Countess Maria Theresa Erdödy on 11 January 1763, the Prince ordered three

The Esterházy Palace
today. A photograph

days of celebrations on a scale even more lavish than those for his own installation the previous year. For this occasion Haydn composed his first full-length opera, *Acide*, which was performed on the first day after lunch. This opera was based on the same story as Handel's *Acis and Galatea* which tells of the love of Acis for the nymph Galatea and his murder by the jealous giant Polyphemus. The cast of five singers was drawn from the choir at Eisenstadt. Haydn directed the performance and the orchestra appeared for the first time in their splendid new Esterházy livery of dark red with gold lacing. Another opera, a comedy by a now forgotten composer, was given on the third day.

From 1763 to 1766, the daily routine at Eisenstadt passed without many activities of note, although the industrious Haydn was constantly busy. It was during this time that Haydn's father Mathias died on 12 September 1763 so severing the composer's last link with any home but that at Eisenstadt.

In 1765 he compiled (together with his copyist, Joseph Elssler [Senior]) the first of a number of lists of his compositions written over the previous fifteen years. This *Entwurfkatalog* (or rough sketch catalogue) reveals the enormous quantity of music he had completed even by that date. It includes thirty symphonies,

34

Haydn's *Entwurfkatalog*, 1765. Autograph of the second page (Berlin, Offentliche Wissenschaftliche Bibliothek)

eighteen string quartets, eighteen string trios and numerous divertimenti, cassations and other casual and occasional works provided mostly for the Esterházy household.

In addition to the symphonies, Haydn also began to write concertos but he did not take to this musical form as willingly or

Archbishop Sigismund
Schrattenbach of
Salzburg (1698–1771)

Michael Haydn (1737–
1806)

successfully as he did to the symphony. In 1762 he composed a
Horn Concerto for one of the players at Eisenstadt; the Violin
Concerto in C of 1765 was written for Tomasini, the leader of his
orchestra. The Cembalo Concerto in F of the same year was
probably played by himself but its unspectacular solo part suggests
that he was reluctant to display his own performing skill. 1765
was also the year in which his brother, Johann Evangelist, joined
the company of singers as a tenor. Haydn's other brother, Michael,
had been appointed musical director to Archbishop Sigismund of
Salzburg in 1762 and remained for the rest of his life in that city,
becoming a close friend of the Mozart family.

The Parterre d'Eau in
the Gardens of Versailles

Chapter 5

Esterháza I

'Words cannot describe how both eye and ear are delighted here'—
Beschreibung des Hochfürstlichen Schlosses Esterhász (1784).

During the year 1764, Prince Nicholas paid a visit to Paris and
was so impressed with the splendour of the palace and gardens of
Versailles that he resolved to establish his own Versailles in
Hungary. The place he selected caused many sceptics to consider
his plan utterly absurd. The proposed site was at that time a
waterlogged forest at Sütter, beside Lake Neusiedler, which often
flooded the surrounding land.

   Before the palace could be built, the whole area had to be
drained and dams constructed. The building itself was erected in
a remarkably short time and was ready for occupation in 1766,
although much work continued to be done in the gardens until as
late as 1784 when the elaborate system of artificial waterfalls and
fountains was completed in front of the main building. The total
cost of this lavish undertaking was eleven million florins, equal to

The Castle of
Esterháza. Contem-
porary engraving (from
*Beschreibung des
Hochfürstlichen Schlosses
Esterhász,* 1784)

nearly two million pounds or nearly four million dollars.

When the castle of Esterháza, as it was called, was finished, the prince wrote the text for an illustrated book (published in Pressburg in 1784) describing the wonders of the place. In addition to the elegant architectural magnificence of the building, the library contained 75,000 books and manuscripts. The art gallery was filled with Italian and Dutch paintings which are today housed in the Budapest Museum of Fine Arts: one of the treasures was a painting of the Madonna by Raphael.

The theatre had seating for 400 and was equipped with intricate lighting effects and stage machinery. The marionette theatre was built like a grotto. As the guide book says:

The walls and niches are covered with different coloured stones, sea shells and snails which strangely reflect the light. The puppets are beautifully made and magnificently dressed: they perform not only in farces and comedies but also in *opera seria*. The performances at both theatres are open to everybody.

The gardens were elaborately laid out without regard to physical obstacles or expense:

Art and nature are here combined in a noble and magnificent manner. In every corner there is something to catch the eye: statues, temples, grottoes and fountains.

In the castle, there were two large halls for the assembled

company, in one of which the concerts were given. The one hundred and twenty-six guest rooms were all designed in the most extravagant style. Life at Esterháza resembled that of the world of the paintings of Watteau, with its life of perpetual pleasure for the aristocracy, a life filled with hunting parties, outdoor festivities, opera and other amusements.

The Prince became preoccupied with improving this luxurious place, so that he spent much of his time there, although originally Esterháza had been intended as a summer residence only. Eisenstadt, on the other hand, was a much more suitable place to occupy in the winter months as it was free from the hazards to health still likely to arise at Esterháza although the swamp had been drained. Also Eisenstadt was nearer to Vienna. Haydn frequently complained of the poor climate at Esterháza which affected his health and that of his musicians who were often sick as a result of the dampness.

When Werner died in 1766, Haydn was appointed *Kapellmeister* and, on his advice, the orchestra was augmented to twenty-two players and the company of singers expanded so that the finest musicians available from as far away as Italy were engaged. In this way, Haydn was able to command the very highest standards, and the fame of Esterháza as the home of excellent music spread throughout Europe.

Also in 1766 Haydn composed a comic opera *La cantarina* (*The Songstress*). The two parts of this were intended to be performed during the intervals in a serious opera or play. The plot concerns Gasparina, a singer who tries to capture the attention of two lovers at the same time. The resulting problems of attempting to please them both without allowing them to discover her duplicity provides a sequence of awkward and amusing situations.

It was staged the following year at Carnival time on 16 February in the presence of the Empress Maria Theresia at Pozsony, now called Bratislava, in Czechoslovakia. The performance took place in a building in the garden of the Bishop's Palace, and it seems that Haydn with the orchestra and the singers must have travelled from Eisenstadt for this one event, a distance of nearly fifty miles. It is probable that the opera had already been performed at Eisenstadt soon after it had been composed.

On the evening of 15 February, Prince Esterházy had entertained his fellow aristocratic guests by giving them a recital on his favourite instrument, the baryton.

For the grand opening of the new opera house at Esterháza in the autumn of 1768, Haydn composed another *opera buffa* called *Lo speziale* (*The Apothecary*). It is based on a libretto by the Italian playwright Goldoni, in which the heroine Grilletta is faced by three suitors: one of them Sempronio, the aged apothecary, is her guardian. The text makes fun of contemporary newspapers for their fanciful and improbable stories in which Sempronio has implicit faith. Mengone, the apothecary's assistant eventually wins Grilletta's hand but is almost beaten to it by Volpino, the third lover, a part sung according to eighteenth century tradition by a soprano dressed as a man. *Lo speziale* is the earliest of Haydn's operas to stand up to present day standards of operatic performance and contains much delightful music and witty dialogue.

Today only the ruins of the opera house remain, but from contemporary prints and cross-section plans, it is possible to visualise many of its features. Although called the opera house, it was also used for most of the dramatic productions as well as opera. It was sixty feet wide and over two hundred feet long. The outside of the building was classical in design and had a gallery supported by Ionic pillars across the façade, with five large french windows which led into the first floor rooms. The mansard roof

Esterháza, the opera house. An original cross-section plan

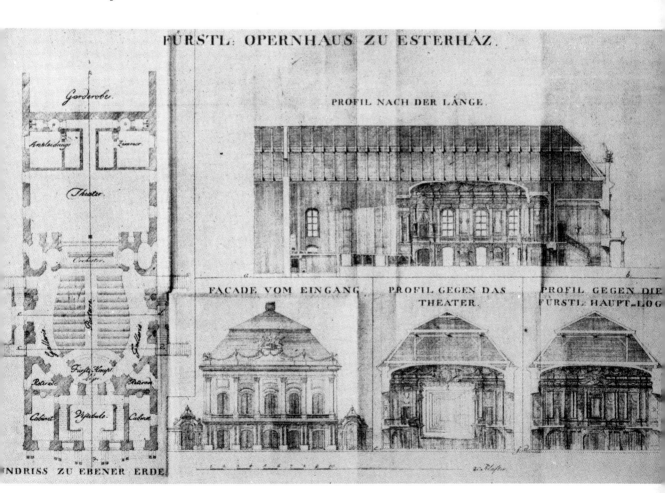

FÜRSTL. OPERNHAUS ZU ESTERHÁZ.

PROFIL NACH DER LÄNGE.

FAÇADE VOM EINGANG   PROFIL GEGEN DAS THEATER.   PROFIL GEGEN DIE FÜRSTL. HAUPT-LOG

NDRISS ZU EBENER ERDE

Haydn. Oil painting by
Ludwig Guttenbrunn
(Wolfgang von
Karajan, Salzburg)

along the whole length of the building provided a roof space
almost as high again as the side walls.

In the auditorium, the Prince's box was on the first floor in the
centre of the balcony facing the stage, with a box on either side.
These were occupied by the distinguished guests who had easy
access to the lavishly furnished rooms behind. There was seating
on the ground floor for about four hundred persons. Down the
whole length of the side walls, on ground level, there were windows
and doors.

The stage space was quite large in comparison to the dimensions
of the auditorium. The width of the proscenium arch was about
thirty-five feet with a depth of stage of nearly forty feet. Behind
the stage were ample dressing rooms and a wardrobe room. The

scenery at the back of the stage was prepared on movable frames mounted on castors. In this way changes of scene could be effected in a matter of seconds. The backcloth could also be replaced with great rapidity.

The stage machinery included a device for raising or lowering actors and singers when a character had to appear out of the sky or be seen to fly away, as was frequently the case in operas and plays on classical subjects. The lighting effects were created by means of oil lamps and mirrors.

One interesting detailed plan which has survived reveals the heating system of the opera house. There were four large stoves at the side of the building, stoked from outside and four more in the basement which radiated heat through holes in the middle of the auditorium floor.

The puppet theatre was opened in 1773 on a site opposite the opera house and separated from it by a garden laid out in the French style. Although the original plans have been lost, it is known that basically it resembled the opera house in its exterior design. The auditorium was on a single floor without boxes or a gallery. The walls were covered with coloured stones and sea-shells which reflected the light from the chandeliers. Behind the stage the actors and singers were concealed from the view of the audience.

Although Haydn and his orchestra played frequently at Esterháza after the opening of the opera house in 1768, the musicians did not move to live there permanently until the following year when the Music House was completed. This building was erected next to the opera house and is one of the few parts of the huge Esterháza palace to remain standing today almost unaltered, although it has been unoccupied for over a century.

The two-story music house is rectangular in shape enclosing three courtyards. With the surviving plans, there is a detailed description of the precise use made of each of the ninety-six rooms. In spite of the size of the building, only Haydn, Tomasini and two senior singers, Friberth and Dichtler were permitted to have their wives living with them. In addition to the musicians and singers, the music house also had to provide accommodation for artists, actors and other servants of the Esterházy household, Haydn's own living area comprised only three rooms and many of the other residents had to share apartments.

From 1761 to 1765, the orchestra at Eisenstadt gave regular performances, usually two a week on the afternoons of Tuesday and Saturday. These concerts lasted about two hours and it is certain that almost all the music played was by Haydn.

After the set of three symphonies, *Le Matin*, *Le Midi* and *Le Soir*, which were his first pieces for the Esterházy orchestra, Haydn continued to compose four or five symphonies each year. In most of these early symphonies frequent use is made of solo instruments, especially in the expressive slow movements. It no doubt pleased the individual players whenever they could display their talents for the Prince to hear. Tomasini, the leader of the orchestra, and Joseph Weigl, an accomplished cellist, who were both only in their twenties seemed to be particularly favoured by the composer in the opportunities given them for technical demonstration of their instruments.

From 1761, the year of his appointment, until 1765, Haydn composed over twenty symphonies. In addition, the Italian style overture to *Acide*, the opera written in 1762, is in the typical three movement form of the genre and could almost be considered a symphony. Any increase in orchestral personnel naturally affected the scoring which Haydn employed in these works. Therefore the employment of two additional horn players in 1763 is reflected in Symphony No. 13 in D, composed in that year for a wind section of flute, two oboes and *four* horns, with the addition of timpani, an innovation for the composer. Four horns are again used in Symphony No. 31, also in D, appropriately subtitled the *Horn-signal* by someone in the nineteenth century. In this elaborate work dating from 1765 (autograph), the horns and indeed all the wind instruments are given virtuoso parts which even by today's high standards of orchestral playing offer considerable technical difficulties to the players. Symphony No. 72, again in D, and probably written between 1761 and 1763 in spite of its late numbering, also has parts for the four horns.

Haydn's post entailed numerous duties sufficient to keep two or three men occupied all their time. He had to rehearse the orchestra and singers every day for regular performances. In addition, his administrative tasks were an important part of his work which must have taken up much of his time and energy. When we see the extent of these, it seems surprising that he succeeded in finding spare moments in which to compose the music which was required.

Haydn discharged these obligations with remarkable success. He had a natural gift for dealing with the day to day problems and disputes amongst his musicians. He earned a considerable respect from them and it is clear that he amply fulfilled the terms of the second clause in his contract, whereby he was to set a good example of conduct towards the players. It was this fatherly care which he took that gained for him the nick-name *Papa*, a title which remained with him to the end of his life.

Christoph Willibald
Gluck (1714–87),
Haydn's great German
contemporary whose
Italian and French
operas were the talk of
Europe. Painting by
Joseph-Sifré de
Duplessis, 1775

Amongst the numerous documents in the Esterházy archives,
there are many letters written by Haydn to the Prince or his
administrator which testify to the composer's deep concern for the
welfare of his musicians. On many occasions he had to intercede on
their behalf to prevent their being punished or dismissed for minor
misdemeanours. For example, in January 1769, Haydn had to
act as peacemaker between the Prince and a tenor in the choir,
Karl Friberth. It was the custom for any person of the Esterházy
household who wished to get married to ask the Prince for formal

Gluck's *Orfeo ed Euridice,* the title page of the first edition, 1764. Engraving by Charles Monnet. In its original Italian form this opera was produced at the Burgtheater in Vienna on 5 October 1762.

permission. When the Prince learnt that Friberth was intending to marry the soprano Magdalena Spangler and had not sought permission, he immediately dismissed both singers.

Haydn intervened and somehow placated the Prince, with the result that neither Friberth nor his bride left Esterháza. Haydn's sympathies must have been particularly roused on this occasion since Magdalena Spangler was the daughter of J. M. Spangler, that very same man who had taken the boy Haydn into his lodging in 1749 after he had been expelled from St. Stephen's. It is probable that Haydn had a hand in obtaining a music post for Friberth in Vienna in 1776.

Chapter 6

Sturm und Drang

'Art is free, and should be fettered by no . . . mechanical regulations. The educated ear is the sole authority on all these questions, and I think I have as much right to lay down the law as anyone'—Haydn

In 1766 Prince Nicholas moved into the palace at Esterháza although much of it was incomplete. Until the music house was finished two years later, the musicians travelled between Eisenstadt and Esterháza, although they must have spent most of their time at the latter.

With the move to Esterháza Haydn's output of symphonies diminished so that from 1766 to 1770 he completed less than ten. A partial explanation for this is that with the death of Werner, Haydn probably felt able for the first time to write church music without incurring the old man's jealousy as most of the church music played hitherto at Eisenstadt had been by Werner. If this is the case, it again shows the younger man's respect for the aged *Kapellmeister* and his tact in deliberately avoiding a cause for rivalry.

In 1766, the year of Werner's death, Haydn wrote his first religious work for the Prince, the *Missa in honorem Beata Maria Virgine* (Mass in honour of the Blessed Virgin Mary), also known as the Great Organ Mass in E flat. It is scored for four soloists, chorus and an orchestra of two cor anglais, bassoon, two horns and strings with an important part for organ, hence its secondary title. The following year he composed a setting of the *Stabat Mater* for almost identical forces.

Esterháza also revived in Haydn the interest he had once possessed in the string quartet. After a silence in this medium for about ten years, he composed between 1768 and 1772 in fairly quick succession the three sets, each of six quartets, published as Op. 9, Op. 17, and Op. 20. The reason for this renewed attention cannot be definitely established, but the baryton trios which Haydn had been obliged to provide for the Prince were becoming less required by him so that Haydn's interest in instrumental music naturally transferred itself to the string quartet. He may

Symphony No. 29.
Manuscript page of the
first violin part in the
hand of Joseph Elssler
(senior), official music
copyist to Prince
Esterházy; c. 1765–70
(Monastery of St. Florian,
Upper Austria)

also have wished to make further use of the two gifted players,
Tomasini and Weigl, whose technical ability was already being
exploited in the symphonies composed at this time.

The first two years at Esterháza produced only a handful of
symphonies, of which No. 59 in A (the so-called *Fire* Symphony)
was probably based on incidental music for a play. Then during
the years 1768 to 1770, Haydn's orchestral works underwent a
marked change. Throughout Central Europe at this time, but
especially in Germany, a new wave of literature suddenly became

very popular and its influence was soon felt in both music and the visual arts. This movement was given the name *Sturm und Drang* (*Storm and Stress*) for it revealed especially in poetry an intensely emotional character quite alien to the previous nature of eighteenth century literature. The poetry and prose of the *Sturm und Drang* school conveyed a passionate melancholy more akin to the romanticism of the following century.

Although the term *Sturm und Drang* comes from a play written in 1776 by the German dramatist Friedrich Maximilian von Klinger (1752–1831), the movement now bearing that title swept through Germany many years earlier. One possible source of this revolutionary romanticism of gloom and despair may have been the widespread performances in new German translations of Shakespeare's tragedies. Both *Hamlet* and *Macbeth* were produced at Esterháza in 1773 and revived the following year when *King Lear* and *Othello* were also added to the repertoire. In 1776 a visiting company performed *Richard III* and *Romeo and Juliet*. Haydn, it has been claimed, composed music for *Hamlet* but it

Johann Wolfgang von Goethe (1749–1832), perhaps the greatest *Sturm und Drang* poet of the age; his epistolary novel, *Die Leiden des jungen Werthers* appeared in 1774. Engraving by J. H. Lips

has not survived in this form,* although some of it may well have been incorporated into other works at a later date.

Not surprisingly, *Sturm und Drang* elements do not appear in Haydn's operas, since such dark moods would hardly have pleased an aristocratic audience whose tastes in opera and theatre were strictly limited to a whole range of Italian comedies and classical tragedies remote from genuine feelings.

As a result the first work in which this deeply emotional though not necessarily personal intensity is felt turns out to be a symphony—No. 26 in D minor, *Lamentatione*. The subtitle, apparently authentic, was given to this piece since the slow movement is based on a plainsong chant from the *Lamentations* of Jeremiah at the words 'Here begins the lamentations of the Prophet Jeremiah'. The opening movement has a subsidiary tune derived from an old Austrian melody of the Middle Ages associated with the Passion of Easter. It is possible that Haydn composed the symphony for performance shortly before Easter which would explain the tragic mood of the music.

Symphony No. 39 in G minor, also composed in 1768, has a similarly driving intensity and tragedy which was to be imitated by Mozart in the first of his two symphonies in the same key, No. 25, K. 183, written some five years later. Interestingly, Haydn uses four horns, two each in B flat and G, so that between them they can cover the arpeggio of G minor without difficulty. Mozart, in his Symphony No. 25, likewise employed four horns in the same way; the device was, of course, less to increase the volume of sound than to accommodate the fact that the horn then was a natural, non-chromatic instrument 'crooked' in various *major* keys. Compared with modern valve instruments, the range of available pure or 'open' notes was limited, the more so in a *minor* key context; accordingly, in order to get more notes in a piece written in the minor key one simply had to use several horns crooked in different keys.**

In the last movement of this same symphony Haydn gives his violins a number of wide leaps in quick succession of over two octaves which imbue the music with an element of frantic despair. This feature appears again in the persistently troubled mood of the second movement of another contemporaneous symphony, No. 49 in F minor, subtitled *La Passione* because it was first performed during Holy Week. The last movement, incidentally,

* A manuscript source of doubtful authenticity was reported to have been found at the Benedictine Abbey of Göttweig shortly before the 1939-45 War

** *cf* comments on the trumpet, p. 125.

Symphony No. 49.
Autograph page
(Stockholm Royal
Swedish Musical
Academy)

has a fierceness which even the connection with the Passion cannot adequately explain. Its strangely violent nature seems indeed to portray a passion which was perhaps more essentially personal than religious in derivation. If this really was the case, then *La Passione* must be one of those very rare works in Haydn's output in which something of himself was actually allowed to colour the overall mood and dramatic tension (he seldom ever, after all, confused the job of creating music with the traumas and troubles of his own life; later generations instead were left to savour that conflict).

Another notable work on the *Sturm und Drang* period was the Symphony No. 44 in E minor, composed about three years later in 1771. It subsequently acquired the title *Trauer* or *Mourning* as Haydn requested that the slow movement should be played at his own funeral.

The last work by Haydn to belong to this particularly emotional phase during the middle years of his stay at Esterháza, was his Symphony No. 45. It is perhaps among the best known of his works mainly on account of the true story associated with its unusual last movement. Written in 1772, and in the remote key of F sharp minor, it was, in fact, this finale that prompted the nickname *Farewell* some time in the last quarter of the eighteenth century. Never has a title been more apt. The circumstances of it all lay, of course, with the Esterházy musicians who, though they might well have found their work congenial, especially with so understanding a *Kapellmeister*, still managed to harbour one grievance. Their accommodation, in fact, was not large enough for them to have their families with them, and except for Haydn and three senior members, all of them had to live away from their wives for the greater part of the year.

When the summer of 1772 passed and it seemed that the Prince would not make his customary visit to Vienna, the players became restless at the prospect of not seeing their families at all that year. They appealed to Haydn who had the characteristically subtle idea of conveying their unrest to the Prince by way of a musical joke.

The symphony has the usual four movements with a minuet in the distant and hitherto almost unused key of F sharp major. At the end of the fourth movement the music reaches a conclusion in the key of C sharp instead of the expected F sharp. At this point, Haydn adds an *Adagio* in order to bring home to his patron the mood of the musicians. The music is scored in such a way that as each instrument in turn finishes his part, the player puts out his candle, gathers his music and quietly departs, leaving only two violins still playing at the end of the work. Fortunately without anger, the Prince took the hint that the musicians were eager to get away for a holiday. The next day he gave orders for the company to prepare for immediate departure for Vienna where most of the orchestra had their homes.

An interesting document which throws considerable light upon Haydn's performances of his own works is a set of instructions he wrote for a performance of a choral work entitled *Applausus*. This festive cantata, written in 1768, was commissioned for the inaugu-

An opera performance at Esterháza. H. C. Robbins Landon has suggested that on the basis of stage settings and costumes the painting probably depicts a scene from Haydn's 'Turkish' opera, *L'incontro improviso* (1775). Haydn is at the cembalo, and a cellist and two bass players are reading from his score. Also to be seen are a bassoonist, two oboists, thirteen violin and viola players, and a kettledrum (V. E. Pollak Collection, Vienna)

ration of a new prelate at the monastery of Zwettl in Lower Austria. As the composer could not be present at the ceremony, he sent detailed notes on how he wanted the music played.

He asked that all marks of tempo and dynamics should be carefully followed with clear contrasts made between piano and pianissimo, and forte and fortissimo, and that similar attention should be given to phrasing. He required that the recitatives should follow the arias without a break, and that the singers should deliver the words slowly so that every syllable could be understood easily. Regarding the instrumentation he asked for two viola players since their part was independent of the bass line. Haydn also recommended that a bassoon should reinforce the cellos and double basses.

The experience of the composer as a director of music is seen also in the request he made for the copyist to make certain that the violinists did not all turn over their pages at the same point in the work as this would reduce the volume of string tone. Finally, he urged that there should be at least four rehearsals so that the musicians would be completely familiar with their parts.

It is evident from these instructions that Haydn took meticulous

care over the music he prepared and expected others to do like-wise, especially when he was not able to supervise the performance himself.

On 22 March 1770 the Esterházy orchestra and singers made their first appearance in Vienna. They performed Haydn's opera *Lo speziale* in the private home of an Austrian nobleman, Gottfried Freiherr von Sumerau. This performance was considered the most significant musical event of the season.

Later that year, on 16 September, a large party of guests at Esterháza attended the first performance of another opera *Le pescatrici* (*The Fishermaids*) which had been composed by Haydn the previous year to mark the wedding of Prince Esterházy's niece, Countess Lamberg, to Count Pozzi. In this *opera buffa*, to a libretto by Goldoni, Haydn combines comic and serious dramatic elements. The serious characters, Prince Lindoro and his bride, Eurilda, sing formal elaborate arias; the comic figures, two fishermen and their lovers are given much simpler songs with folk-song features. In contrast to his previous operas, Haydn makes frequent use of ensembles in *Le pescatrici*, including a septet in the first act.

After the first performance, the Prince entertained his visitors with an elaborate display on stage by his grenadiers. These soldiers enacted battle scenes with such noise and realism that Haydn's music must have been completely annihilated from the memory of the audience by the subsequent military spectacle.

To honour the name day of the Dowager Princess Marie Louise, widow of Prince Anton Esterházy, the première of Haydn's new opera *L'infedeltà delusa* (*Unfaithfulness Deluded*) was given on 26 July 1773. The rather feeble plot is concerned with the power of love which overcomes all obstacles. After the performance, the whole palace and the grounds were brilliantly illuminated and the company were entertained to a fancy dress ball.

When the Empress Maria Theresia paid a visit to Esterháza in the following September, the opera was repeated for her benefit. The Empress is reported to have declared that whenever she wished to hear opera well performed, she would travel to Esterháza. If this remark is authentic, the Empress intended it merely as a compliment since she never went there again during her life.

Also to entertain the Empress, a puppet opera with music by Haydn, *Philemon and Baucis* was performed. It is probable that this was the first production to be mounted in the newly built puppet theatre. For over a century, the music for this piece had been lost, but much of it in an old manuscript version with spoken dialogue was discovered in 1950 in the Paris Conservatoire Library.

Haydn. Engraving
by Johann Ernest
Mansfeld, 1781

Exemple maiestueux d'examiner tout et d'encourager les
Sujets a Diligence donné par l'Empereur Joseph II.
le 19. Aout 1769. en Moravie.

Chapter 7

Esterháza II

'His mixture of serious and comic is disliked; particularly as there is more of the latter than the former in his work and as for rules, he knows but little of them'—quoted by Dr. Burney

Emperor Joseph II instructing a peasant in the art of plowing. Engraving, 1769. Joseph II (1741–80) succeeded to the Austrian throne in 1765, and ruled the Habsburg Empire jointly with his mother, the Dowager Empress Maria Theresia. He became King of Bohemia and Hungary on her death in 1780. An ally of Catherine the Great of Russia, his incognito adventures have made him in a popular legend 'a sort of modern Harun-al-Rashid'. Both Gluck and Mozart held ill-paid posts at his court

Life continued at Esterháza without much change. Almost every year saw the arrival of some very important guest for whom elaborate entertainments were provided. The Empress Maria Theresia's visit in 1773 must have reminded Haydn of the episode when as a boy he climbed the scaffolding at her palace at Schönbrunn. This time however the Empress was certainly pleased with the composer and presented him with a valuable gold snuff-box which was filled with ducats. As well as the opera and puppet opera performed in her honour, Haydn revived his Symphony No. 48 in C, composed in 1769, which acquired the appellation *Maria Theresia*. It was played at a concert in the Chinese Pavilion.

During the next decade, Haydn's major works were in the field of opera, although he also composed two important choral pieces, the *St. Cecilia* Mass, completed in about 1772, and his first oratorio, *The Return of Tobias*. This latter work was written in 1774–75 for the Society of Music in Vienna, an example of his contravening the terms of his original contract by providing music for performance outside Esterháza. The concert at which it was given was organised to raise money for poor musicians and their families who benefitted by 2,000 florins, a considerable sum of money at that time. In spite of this success, it was many years afterwards that Haydn made any great impression upon the musical élite of Vienna.

Still the duties at Esterháza occupied most of his time and energies. For the visit of Archduke Ferdinand and the Archduchess Beatrice d'Este in August 1775, Haydn wrote a comic opera *L'incontro improviso* (*The Unexpected Meeting*) on a Turkish theme very similar to that of Mozart's later *Il Seraglio*.* The vogue for Turkish music and art was beginning to grow in Germany and

* See illustration on p. 53.

The Great Siege of
Vienna by the Turks,
1683. This contemporary
engraving shows the
final battle (on 12
September) when the
Imperial Army appeared
to relieve the capital

Opposite
The Monastery of St.
Florian, Upper Austria.
Engraving by Vischer,
c. 1674. Haydn himself
maintained a close
connection with this
monastery, and to this
day it has remained a
repository of some
valuable and even
unique manuscript
scores. As Landon has
observed, the Austro-
German-Czech
monasteries in general
'provide us with the
greatest quantity of
existing Haydn sources,
and a part of his music
has survived only in
copies preserved in these
far-flung collections'

Austria now that the tragic memory of Turkish domination of
parts of the Austro-Hungarian Empire was fading away.

In this same year, Haydn completed the Mass *St. Joanni de Deo*
(*St. John of God*) in B flat which is also known as the *Little Organ
Mass* to distinguish it from the earlier Organ Mass in E flat. Also
in 1775 Prince Nicholas finally lost all interest in the baryton, so
that he required no more divertimenti to be written for the
instrument.

In the following year a fire at Eisenstadt destroyed a number of
Haydn's manuscripts, as a similar fire had done in 1768; precisely
what was lost on either occasion is not known. Arising out of the
success in Vienna of *The Return of Tobias*, Haydn was asked to
compose an opera *La vera constanza* (*True Constancy*). With the
Imperial Opera Company resources in mind, he planned the
work on an ambitious scale. Unfortunately, Haydn experienced
difficulties in finding a suitable cast and was so infuriated by petty
intrigues against him and a general lack of co-operation, that
he withdrew the opera from its proposed production. It was
eventually staged at Esterháza in 1779.

Between 1776 and 1779, he composed three more operas. However, the first of these, *Die Feuerbrunst oder das Abgebrannte Haus*
(*The Conflagration or the Burned House*) was probably performed in
the puppet threatre, and was really more in the nature of incidental music. In spite of the title, this is a comedy, indeed somewhat a farce including a clown, a dragon and a ghost among the
cast. The music is said to have been based on Symphony No. 59
(*c.* 1766–68).

Another and better documented incident took place that year (1776) on 24 October during a performance of Telemann's opera *Il finto pazzo per amore*. The tenor Bendetto Bianchi played a trick on the soprano Katharina Poschwa by twice lifting up the edge of her skirt with his stick. Although she herself was not at first aware of this, the audience, which included her husband, objected strongly. After a complaint was presented to the Prince, Bianchi was sentenced to a public whipping and two weeks in prison. He also had to present an apology for the offence at his next appearance on stage.

For the wedding of Prince Nicholas Esterházy, second son of the ruling Prince, and Countess Maria Anna Weissenwolf on 3 August 1777, Haydn wrote another Italian opera, *Il Mondo della Luna* (*The Land of the Moon*). Like *Lo speziale*, the libretto was based on a story by Goldoni. It concerns Buonafede who is over-enthusiastic about astronomy. Two suitors for his daughters trick him into thinking he has been transported to the moon.

Harpsichord by Burkat
Shudi the Elder and
John Broadwood,
London 1775. Haydn
acquired this instrument
two years after Shudi's
death for use at
Esterháza (Vienna,
Kunsthistorisches
Museum)

They succeed in obtaining his approval of their marriages by
pretending that they are important moon beings. The overture
was later used as the first movement of Symphony No. 63 (*c.*
1777–80).

In 1777 Haydn paid 2,000 gulden for a house at Eisenstadt. It
was here that he intended to live when the Esterházy court
moved to Eisenstadt each winter. The following year there arose
the first rumours that Haydn had died. The origin of this false
report is not known, but the story reached England where Dr.
Charles Burney recorded the death of Haydn in his *General History
of Music* published at the end of that year.

The eventual première of *La vera constanza* took place in the
spring of 1779. As in the case of *L'incontro improviso*, this *dramma
giocoso* again offers us a number of remarkable parallels with a
Mozart work as then unwritten, this time *The Marriage of Figaro*
(1786). The heroine is named Rosina who marries a count and is

subjected to a number of indignities by her husband who wrongly suspects her of infidelity. In these features both characters and situations are similar to their counterparts in Mozart's opera.

In *La vera constanza* Haydn makes frequent use of recitative accompanied by the orchestra instead of the usual harpsichord continuo. Recitatives and arias often follow each other without any breaks so that long sequences of continuous music are built up, comprising as many as nine linked sections. After the initial performances at Esterháza, the opera was produced in Pressburg (now Brno in Czechoslovakia) in 1785, in Vienna in 1790 and in Paris the following year.

For his next opera, Haydn chose a text by Metastasio, then aged eighty-one, who had helped the young composer twenty years earlier in Vienna. *L'isola disabitata* (*The Uninhabited Island*) had served as a libretto for several operas by other composers including Holzbauer and Jommelli. This work shows clearly the influence of Gluck with all the recitatives accompanied by the orchestra and the use of recurring thematic motifs. The simple subject is treated almost in a classical manner with little action. Constanza, the heroine, has been separated from her husband, Ernesto, but after living on a desert island, where she has been abandoned by pirates, she is reunited with him.

L'isola disabitata was the first opportunity Haydn had for writing music for a newly recruited nineteen-year old singer, Luigia Polzelli, a mezzo, whose husband Antonio had been engaged as a violinist in 1779. Antonio Polzelli was considerably older than his wife and was suffering from consumption. Their marriage was clearly not a happy one and Haydn, whose own matrimonial life was a failure, took an affectionate interest in the attractive girl. Since he was twenty-eight years her senior, we can assume that his feelings were at first paternal and protective.

Although little is known about Luigia, she seems later to have provided the composer with a renewed happiness. Although her singing voice was not distinguished, Haydn took great pains to transpose arias for her and to simplify difficulties she could not overcome. She played only minor rôles in the operas at Esterháza, which Haydn often adapted to suit her capabilities. Her initial contract at the Esterházy Court was for only one year, but although the Prince wished to dismiss the Polzellis in 1780, they remained in employment there, no doubt through the intercession of Haydn.

Before *L'isola disabitata* could be given its première in the large theatre at Esterháza, the building was destroyed by fire on the night of 18 November 1779. The Chinese Pavilion next to it was being made ready for the wedding celebrations of Count Anton

Forgach and Countess Grassalkovich on 21 November. Two large stoves which had been kept alight for several days to heat the rooms probably exploded. The fire spread rapidly to the adjoining theatre which was completely gutted in half an hour. But for a heavy shower of rain, other buildings, including the castle itself, might have been severely damaged. Once again, Haydn lost a number of scores as a result of fire.

This disaster did not upset arrangements for the wedding which took place three days later as originally planned. All operatic and dramatic performances were transferred to the puppet theatre where on 6 December Haydn's opera was given its première less than three weeks after the fire.

The Prince's determination to restore the opera and theatre to its original place with as little interruption as possible is shown by the fact that on 18 December, exactly one month after the blaze, the foundation stone was laid for a new opera house. Completely new foundations were erected and within ten months the opera house was finished in a style even more lavish than its predecessor. Although it was used in November 1780 for the performance of plays, Haydn's opera *La fedeltà premiata* (*Faithfulness Rewarded*) intended for the official opening ceremony on 15 October had to be postponed since the stage was not ready for operatic productions.

The opera was eventually heard in the following February. This pastoral comedy has a weak and naive plot with two shepherds as the central figures. The prelude to the third act, scored for rustic oboes, bassoons, horns, trumpets, drums and strings, was used again by Haydn as the finale to his Symphony No. 73 in D (*La Chasse*), composed in 1781.

About this time, the Prince's enthusiasm for opera increased, perhaps as a result of his loss of interest in playing the baryton. As a result, Haydn was required to conduct three operatic performances a week instead of the two which had been the previous practice. This inevitably meant that time devoted to composition was further reduced.

Haydn's reputation had spread rapidly by the late 1770's although he was still confined for almost the whole time at Esterháza. He himself referred to his existence there as being 'buried alive', although this comment did not mean that he was unhappy. In 1781 Le Gros, the director of the *Concerts Spirituels* in Paris, wrote to Haydn expressing delight in the *Stabat Mater* of 1773 which he had performed, and requesting the composer to provide other works. Three years later, another musical organisation in Paris, *Les Concerts de la Loge Olympique*, commissioned six symphonies. For them in 1785-86 Haydn wrote the set now

Symphony No. 85.
Autograph fragment
(Berlin, Öffentliche
Wissenschaftliche
Bibliothek)

known as the *Paris* Symphonies. These include No. 82 in C,
known as *The Bear* because of the drone bass in the last movement,
No. 83 nicknamed *The Hen* from the repeated notes played by the
oboe in the first movement, and No. 85 called *La Reine* as it was a
favourite work of Marie Antoinette. The considerable popularity
of these symphonies led to a request for three more, Nos. 90 to
92, which were composed in 1788, apparently for one Count
d'Ogny.

1781 was also the year in which Haydn made his first contacts
with England through the British Ambassador in Vienna, General
Jermingham. William Forster, a London publisher and violin
maker, had made a request through the ambassador for permission
to issue Haydn's music in England. This led to the publication of
a quantity of the composer's symphonies and a number of other
works. Soon other London publishers followed suit and one of
them, John Bland, even travelled to Esterháza (in 1789) to obtain
new works. One story arising from this visit led to the nickname
Razor being applied to the String Quartet in F minor, Op. 55
No. 2. Haydn was finding difficulty in shaving with a blunt razor
and is reported to have said, 'I would give my best quartet for a
good razor', whereupon Bland immediately gave him his own set
of English steel razors. As good as his word, Haydn presented
Bland with a manuscript of this quartet.

In 1782 three people died who had been associated with Haydn. On 21 April at the age of 84, Metastasio died in Vienna in the house he had occupied since 1735. On 1 May Maria Theresa, the wife of Prince Anton Esterházy. For her wedding in 1763, Haydn had written his first full length opera, *Acide*. The third person to die that year, in July, was Princess Maria Anna Luisa, the widow of Prince Paul Anton Esterházy, who had taken Haydn into his employment in 1761.

Haydn's next opera, *Orlando Paladino*, proved to be the most popular in his life-time, receiving thirty performances at Esterháza in two years, and subsequently produced at thirty-three different opera houses in Germany and Austria before the end of the century. It is possible that the first presentation (in the August of 1782) was given by marionettes in the puppet theatre. Its mixture of tragedy and comedy based on Ariosto's characters of the early sixteenth century would certainly have seemed appropriate for puppet figures.

Haydn's other important work of 1782 was the *Missa Celensis* in C (*The Mass of Mariazell in Styria*), the Benedictus of which was based on a secular aria from *Il mondo della luna*. In composing this Mass for the church at Mariazell, Haydn no doubt recalled his visit there in 1750 when he had been a destitute musician anxiously seeking employment. He was also unlikely to forget the kindness of the choir who on that occasion had organised a collection of money to help him. The year after this work, 1783, the Emperor Joseph II imposed a ban on the use of orchestral

The Palace and Gardens of Versailles, the inspiration of Esterháza

instruments to accompany music *in church*, which was to deter Haydn for nearly fourteen years from writing large scale religious choral works.

Haydn's last two stage works for Esterháza were composed in 1783. For *L'assedio di Gibilterra* (*The Siege of Gibraltar*), a puppet play produced on 20 August 1783, he provided only incidental music. In contrast, the opera *Armida*, first performed on 26 February 1784, he considered to be his finest creation in this medium: 'It is my best work up to now,' he said. In two features *Armida* represents a departure from the style of his previous operas. The overture contains musical ideas from the ensuing opera itself, acting as a symphonic synopsis of the plot. Secondly, Haydn sustains the serious character of the story throughout with no compensating humorous element at all. The story based on Tasso had already been treated as an opera by both Lully and Gluck and by Handel in his *Rinaldo*. Rinaldo, a knight, falls in love with the sorceress Armida but eventually overcomes his passion for her. Over a hundred years later, Dvořák used the same story for his last opera, also called *Armida*.

Ample proof of the neglect into which Haydn's operas fell in the early nineteenth century can be seen in the following conversation from the novel *Gryll Grange* by Thomas Love Peacock, published in 1860. The author, who was one of the most highly educated and informed men of his time, was born in London in 1785. He possessed a considerable knowledge of music and much enjoyed the works of Haydn. Yet in this novel he reveals complete ignorance concerning Haydn's operas.

Mr. Falconer: What say you to Haydn?
Miss Ilex: Haydn has not written operas and my principal experience is derived from Italian theatre. But his music is essentially dramatic.

Chapter 8

Haydn and Mozart

'Most celebrated and very dear friend'—Mozart

It is probable that Haydn and Mozart first met in Vienna in 1781 although there are no details of the circumstances or the date. There grew up between them the very closest friendship with never a trace of envy or rivalry. The enormous respect they possessed for each other's work gave rise to a remarkable understanding. Mozart showed his new compositions to the older man and accepted without reserve any comments made. There was no real teacher-pupil relationship but Mozart certainly valued Haydn's opinion above that of any other musician, even his father.

In temperament and age the two differed considerably; Mozart was the brilliant composer and keyboard virtuoso who wrote music with astounding ease and speed. He was incapable of managing his own financial affairs and seems to have been generally careless in all matters outside the sphere of music. Haydn by contrast was a comparatively slow worker and on his own admission no soloist as a performer, but a meticulous and efficient administrator. In spite of these total divergencies of character, there seems to have been not a single instance of conflict between them.

In 1785 at a private concert in Vienna, Mozart, his father Leopold and two Austrian noblemen played three of the set of six new quartets which Mozart was to dedicate to Haydn who was present to hear them. Afterwards Haydn spoke to Leopold Mozart stating:

> I tell you before God as an honest man that your son is the greatest composer known to me either in person or by reputation. He has taste and what is more the most profound knowledge of composition. (quoted in one of Leopold's letters, 16 February 1785).

Wolfgang Amadeus Mozart (1756–91). Oil painting by Barbara Kraft, 1819 (Vienna, Gesellschaft der Musikfreunde)

Mozart had taken an uncharacteristically long time over these quartets, nearly two years. He held Haydn in such high esteem that only the very best he could produce would be worthy of a

Playbill of the Viennese première of *Don Giovanni*

Playbill of the Viennese première of *Don Giovanni*

The engraved title page of Artaria's first edition of the six quartets that Mozart dedicated to Haydn and published in 1785 as his Opus 10 (Nos. 387, 421, 428, 458, 464 and 465 in Köchel's *Catalogue*)

dedication to Haydn. No other works in his whole output seem to have received such careful attention. In his own words they were 'the fruits of long and arduous toil . . . from Haydn I learnt how to compose a quartet' (preface to the first edition).

Mozart often spoke out in support of Haydn. To Leopold Kozeluch, the Bohemian composer, he said: 'Even if they melted us together, there would still not be enough to make a Haydn.' Haydn, in turn, often made reference to Mozart's neglected genius. After the Viennese première of *Don Giovanni* (7 May 1788), he declared: 'Mozart is the greatest composer the world possesses at this time.'

Until he became acquainted with the operas of Mozart, Haydn had composed works for the stage with some regularity. He had been taking a pride in these and especially in *Armida*, the last composed for Esterháza, but once he recognised the superiority of Mozart's works in this field, without any feeling of jealousy, he lost interest in composing operas.

In the autumn of 1787, Haydn received a request from Prague for a new opera. In reply, he wrote the following letter (1 December) which indicates the power of his feelings towards Mozart with a commendable lack of self-interest.

You ask me to write an *opera buffa* for you. If you have the idea of producing it at Prague, I must decline your request, as all my operas are too closely connected with Esterháza that they could not be performed properly away from that locality.

It would be quite different if I could take pleasure in writing a completely new work for the Prague theatre. But even if this were the case, I should be unable to stand comparison with such a man as Mozart.

If I could tell every music lover and especially the leading musicians of to-day what I feel about the inimitable works of Mozart, their depth of emotion and their unique musical quality, every nation would compete to possess such a great person within its boundaries.

Prague ought to employ this man of worth and to pay him well; for without such reward, every genius is a sad figure, and this gives little encouragement for others to follow his example. In such a way is great talent lost to the world. It troubles me to think that such an unparalleled being as Mozart is not engaged at an imperial or royal court. Please forgive me for forgetting the purpose of this letter, but I love that man so much.

Lorenzo da Ponte
(1749–1838)

Mozart later invited Haydn to the final rehearsals for the première of *Così fan tutte* in Vienna (26 January 1790). Every morning the two composers walked arm in arm to the theatre where it was to be staged.

Shortly after this when Mozart heard that Haydn was intending to visit London he exclaimed, 'But Papa, you have had no education for travelling in the world and you speak so few languages.' Haydn replied, 'My language is understood all over the world.' At about this time, Lorenzo da Ponte, the librettist of Mozart's operas *The Marriage of Figaro*, *Don Giovanni* and *Così fan tutte*, was also planning a visit to England. In 1790 he married an English woman, and for financial reasons left Vienna suddenly, principally to avoid his accumulated debts. He suggested to Mozart that he should join him in making a journey to London, where the two of them could seek their fortune. Somewhat cryptically, the composer said that it was too late for him to undertake such a venture, especially as his wife, Constanza, was ill. One can but wonder how Mozart's life might have changed if he had gone to London at this stage.

Shortly before Haydn left for England (at the end of 1790) he and Mozart met for the last time. Perhaps in the light of his remarks to da Ponte, Mozart already had a foreboding of his own death. This can be seen again in his despairing cry to Haydn: 'I fear, Papa, that this will be our last farewell.' Almost exactly a year later, on 5 December 1791, he was dead. The news of his death reached Haydn in London, but at first he refused to believe that such a catastrophe was true. His own death had been reported several times before. By January of the following year

Mozart, the last portrait.
From a drawing by
Doris Stock, 1789
(Bettman Archive)

Haydn knew that his greatly loved friend was indeed no more.
This tragedy affected him so deeply that years later he was often
moved to tears at the mere mention of Mozart's name. About
his reaction to Mozart's death, he wrote from London the

following letter to a Viennese musical friend and sometime fellow mason*:

I was for some time utterly beside myself about his death. I could not believe that Providence should so suddenly have called such an irreplaceable man into the next world. Have the kindness, dear friend, to send me a list of Mozart's works not known here yet, and I will do all I can to promote them in the interests of his widow. I wrote to the poor woman three weeks ago telling her that when her son is old enough, I shall teach him composition without payment, so as to replace his father as best I can to some small extent.

The simplest tribute Haydn paid to Mozart was made to Dr. Charles Burney in the London music shop of Broderip: 'Friends often flatter me that I have some genius, but he stood far above me.'

* In February 1785, on Mozart's recommendation, Haydn had become a Freemason. His interest in Masonry appears to have been primarily social; probably because of his very strong Catholic faith which opposed certain Masonic practices, he took little part in meetings or ceremonies and resigned in 1787.
Freemasonry in Austria lasted little more than fifty years: the first Vienna Lodge was constituted in 1742 and a National Grand Lodge of the Austrian States was formed in 1789. With the accession of Franz II (1792) Freemasonry began to be discouraged and then more or less died out after an Imperial edict suppressed the Craft in 1795 and made it illegal for anyone to belong to a Lodge.

Chapter 9

Worldly Fame

'My language is understood all over the world'—Haydn

By 1785, Haydn's reputation had reached as far as Spain. From a canon of Cadiz Cathedral, he received a request to compose instrumental music for *The Seven Last Words of Our Saviour From The Cross*. It is probable that Haydn had been recommended by Boccherini, then living in Spain, who had a strong admiration for his works. The music was intended for performance on Good Friday at a special service where the bishop pronounced the seven last sentences of Christ, after each of which the orchestra would play a short instrumental item. The orchestral forces required by the composer are unusually large: double woodwind, four horns, two trumpets, two timpani and strings.

Haydn's response to this commission was to compose seven slow movements which were given their first performance on 26 March 1787. Haydn received payment for the work in a somewhat unusual manner. The Spanish canon sent him a large chocolate cake which was filled with gold coins.

It is interesting to note, by the way, that this work was performed in America as early as 1793. Subsequently, in the late 1790s, Haydn made a choral version of *The Seven Last Words* after he had heard an adaptation of the work, made by the German composer Joseph Friebert, which he considered unsatisfactory. This was performed at Eisenstadt in October 1797. Haydn also made an arrangement for string quartet, the form in which it is most frequently played today. The composer's last appearance in public as a conductor was when he performed the work at a charity concert in Vienna in 1803. The music itself in its vocal version was published in 1801 by the Leipzig company of Breitkopf & Härtel. Haydn provided an explanatory preface:

About fifteen years ago a canon of Cadiz commissioned me to write some pieces of instrumental music on the *Seven Worlds of Christ on the Cross*.

At that time, it was the custom to perform an oratorio in the Cathedral during Lent, and, to give it greater solemnity, it was done with great

Haydn. Gouache by
Johann Zitterer, *c.* 1790

73

The Baryton, the favourite instrument of Prince Nicholas Esterházy I. This particular Austrian example dates from 1779 (New York, Metropolitan Museum of Art, Crosby Brown Collection of Musical Instruments)

pomp. The walls, windows and columns were draped in black, and a single lamp, suspended from the centre, feebly lighted the sanctuary.

At noon the doors were closed and the orchestra began to play. After the introduction, the Bishop mounted his throne, recited one of the *Seven Words* and made some reflections on it. He then descended, kneeled before the altar, and remained thus for some time. This pause was taken up by the music.

The Bishop then mounted and descended six more times, and each time, after his homily, music was heard.

It was to these ceremonies that the music had to adapt itself.

The problem of composing seven *adagios* to be performed consecutively, and lasting ten minutes apiece without fatiguing the congregation, was not an easy one to resolve, and I soon recognised the impossibility of confining my music within the circumscribed limits.

My work was [originally] written and published without words. Later, I had occasion to add them, which is why the *Oratorio*, as now published by Breitkopf & Härtel, is a complete work and, as to the vocal part, altogether new. The good reception it has had among music lovers gives me the hope that the rest of the public will receive it with the same kindness.

Also in 1785, Haydn was asked by King Ferdinand IV of Naples to write music for his favourite instrument the *lyra organizzata*. Just as Prince Nicholas Esterházy had been passionately keen on an obsolete instrument, the baryton, the King of Naples possessed an inordinate enthusiasm for a musical curiosity, the *lyra organizzata*. Like the baryton, it never achieved popularity because of the difficulty in performance. Basically it resembled a hurdy-gurdy, comprising a number of strings which provided a drone and two strings used for the melody. It was operated by a cranking handle attached to a wooden wheel which pressed on the strings somewhat in the manner of a circular bow. A complicated system of keys and wooden arms connected to a set of bellows produced the melodies by blowing air into small pipes like a miniature organ.

The King played duets with his teacher, the Austrian Ambassador in Naples: through his experience in providing numerous baryton trios for Prince Nicholas, Haydn found no difficulty in writing copious concertos and divertimenti for the *lyra*. In present day performance of these pieces, the *lyra* parts are usually allocated to flutes or oboes.

Between 1786 and 1790, Haydn wrote more music for performance outside Esterháza than he did for the use of the Prince, his employer. In addition to the works already mentioned, most of his other important compositions were commissions from abroad. As we have already mentioned, the two sets of symphonies, Nos. 82–87 and 90–92 were composed for performance in Paris, and

not for the orchestra at Esterháza. The important set of six string quartets, published in 1787 as Op. 50, were similarly dedicated to William II of Prussia.

The well-known *Toy Symphony* was published in 1788. At one time attributed to Haydn, it is now generally considered to be by Mozart's father, Leopold. In its gentle humour, the piece would certainly seem to be in accord with Haydn's nature, but he or even his brother, Michael, probably did no more than arrange three movements of a much longer divertimento by Leopold Mozart for strings and toy instruments. The work was thereby ascribed to Leopold. It was, incidentally, performed under Haydn's name in Vienna in 1790 and neither he nor the younger

Mozart himself protested about the authorship.

Haydn's last important works written at Esterháza between 1788 and 1790 were the twelve Quartets which constitute Op. 54, 55 and 64. These were written for Johann Tost, a violinist in the Esterházy Orchestra. In order to flatter the player, all these quartets have a prominent first violin part. After a concert tour abroad, in 1789, the year of the French Revolution and the storming of the Bastille, Tost married a housekeeper at Esterháza and retired from the music profession to become a prosperous Viennese wholesale draper.

Vienna, the Michaelerplatz and the old Imperial Burgtheater. It was here that Mozart's *Seraglio, Figaro* and *Così fan tutte* were first performed. Coloured engraving by C. Postl, *c*. 1805–10

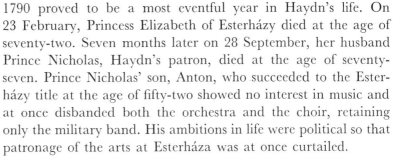

Chapter 10

End of an Era

'It is a sad thing always to be a slave'—Haydn

1790 proved to be a most eventful year in Haydn's life. On 23 February, Princess Elizabeth of Esterházy died at the age of seventy-two. Seven months later on 28 September, her husband Prince Nicholas, Haydn's patron, died at the age of seventy-seven. Prince Nicholas' son, Anton, who succeeded to the Esterházy title at the age of fifty-two showed no interest in music and at once disbanded both the orchestra and the choir, retaining only the military band. His ambitions in life were political so that patronage of the arts at Esterháza was at once curtailed.

Now, like a general without an army, Haydn was granted an annual pension of 1,400 florins and remained technically still in the service of the new prince. He was required therefore to ask the permission of his master before he could undertake any journeys abroad. In this abrupt way, Haydn ended over twenty-nine years of musical service to the Esterházy family. He had few regrets however and had expressed in many letters his growing boredom and frustration with life during these last few years at Esterháza. As a result he had concentrated his greatest efforts upon composing for musical organisations outside the narrow confines of Esterháza.

Haydn at once left to live in Vienna, so eager was he to escape the claustrophobic atmosphere where, in his own words, he had been 'buried alive'. He soon received a request from the King of Naples who was visiting Vienna for the triple wedding of three of his children. King Ferdinand asked Haydn to take up the post of court composer in Naples. The composer was so relieved at the termination of his employment at Esterháza that he was reluctant to accept another such position. The prospect of spending the rest of his life writing music for the *lyra organizzata* must have filled him with horror!

Before he had definitely made up his mind regarding the offer from the King of Naples, Haydn was visited by Johann Peter Salomon, a brilliant violinist who had begun a successful career

Haydn, a silhouette. Engraving by H. Löschenkohl, 'Geist und Harmonie', *Österreichischer Nationalkalender*, 1786

Johann Peter Salomon (1745–1815). Engraving by Facius after the painting by Thomas Hardy, 1792

as a concert promoter. Salomon had been passing through Germany returning to England from a trip to Italy. In Cologne he received news of the death of Prince Nicholas Esterházy. Without delay he turned back to Vienna with the intention of engaging Haydn for a series of concerts in London.

Salomon had been concertmaster to Prince Henry of Prussia and had later lived in Paris. Since 1781 he had been well-established in London as a soloist and leader of an orchestra and also as an impressario. His admiration for Haydn was well known.

Always impetuous and forceful he is said to have introduced himself to the composer in the December of 1790 by saying, 'My name is Salomon; I have come from London to fetch you'. Haydn, who as early as 1787 had written to William Forster, the London music publisher, violin maker and friend of Salomon, expressing his hope of going to England with the intention of giving concerts, accepted this unexpected invitation without hesitation, and on the next day the two men agreed upon the terms of a contract. Haydn was to receive £300 for a new opera, £300 for six new symphonies, and a further £200 for their copyright, £200 for twenty other works and a guarantee of at least £200 from a benefit concert. One can admire the enthusiasm and enterprise of Salomon, prepared to give £1,200 for the services of the composer. It is a matter for regret that such an offer was not made also to Mozart.

Haydn was fifty-eight at this time and had travelled little beyond the environs of Vienna. He had never before even set eyes upon the sea, let alone sailed on a ship, yet the prospect of such a long and arduous journey did not daunt him. His inability to speak a word of English would prove a handicap, but the freedom and adventure presented by the English visit were a greater temptation than the offer from Naples where he would have been familiar with the Italian language which he spoke fluently. Certainly he found difficulty in parting from his many friends in Vienna, who had grave misgivings over the proposed expedition. Those for whom he felt the greatest sorrow in leaving were his beloved Mozart and Marianne von Genzinger, a Viennese lady for whom he had formed a great affection.

On 15 December 1790 Salomon and Haydn set out from Vienna on the first stage of their seventeen-day journey at a time when the French Revolution was still raging. They passed through Munich and arrived in Bonn on Christmas Day. Here they were entertained with a performance of one of Haydn's own masses, and the court musicians, including possibly the twenty-year old Beethoven, laid on a lavish dinner at the Elector's expense. If Beethoven was indeed present, this must have been the first meeting that Haydn had with him although he may already have heard of his talents from Mozart.

On New Year's Eve, the travellers reached Calais where they embarked the following morning for the voyage to Dover. In a letter written that day to Marianne von Genzinger, Haydn boasted that despite his age and lack of experience of the sea, he had withstood the crossing better than most of his companions.

During the first four hours there was hardly any wind and the ship

Ludwig van Beethoven (1770–1827), aged about sixteen in court dress. Silhouette attributed to Neesen (Bonn, Beethoven-Haus)

made very little progress. Fortunately about 11.30 am a strong wind blew us the remaining twenty-two miles and we arrived at 4.0 pm. I stayed on deck throughout the voyage so that I could gaze at the huge monster, the ocean. While there was calm, I had no fear, but when the strong wind blew, increasing every minute, and I saw the violent waves rushing on, I grew alarmed and a little discomposed. But I overcame it all and arrived safely without actually being sick.

From this letter one can see the childlike excitement of the man facing this wholly new experience.

Chapter 11

London: 1791–92

'. . . This great master's genius . . .'—*Gazetteer*, 26 March 1791

Haydn and Salomon reached London on 2 January 1791. They stayed the first night at the house of John Bland, the publisher who had travelled to Esterháza in both 1787 and 1789 to acquire works by Haydn.

The composer was much impressed by the vastness of London. Everything was so different from Vienna. In his diary and in various letters to friends he makes frequent reference to the large numbers of people in the city and the quantity of traffic in the streets. At times he was alarmed at the crush of carriages which almost prevented him from reaching his destination.

To Marianne von Genzinger he wrote on 8 January:

After a tiring journey I am now fresh and well again, and occupied in looking at the endlessly huge city of London, whose various beauties and marvels quite astonish me.

My arrival caused a great sensation throughout the whole city and I was mentioned in all the newspapers for three successive days. Everyone wants to know me. I have had to dine out six times already

London, looking west from London Bridge. Coloured lithograph by W. Daniell, 1805 (British Museum, Crace Collection)

London, the Horse
Guards and Melbourne
House, 1821

Adalbert Gyrowetz
(1763–1850). Engraving
by Mansfeld, 1793

and if I wish, I could dine out every evening. But first I must consider my health and second my work. Except for the nobility, I admit no callers before 2.0 o'clock in the afternoon, and at 4.0 o'clock I dine at home with Mr. Salomon.

I wish I could fly for a time to Vienna to have some quiet in which to work, for the noise in the street is intolerable.

Within a few days of his arrival, Haydn was introduced into the aristocratic circles of London society. He was visited by the Ambassadors of both Austria and Naples, and almost every evening he dined at a different place. He also met the leading literary and musical figures of the capital. The language difficulty caused him much frustration, so that he conscientiously undertook regular English lessons. Salomon and the young Bohemian composer, Adalbert Gyrowetz, a refugee from the French Revolution, who had settled in London two years earlier, acted as interpreters for him. Some of the musicians Haydn met in London he had previously known in Vienna, including Clementi; Stephen Storace, the young English composer; and Jan Ladislav Dussek, the Bohemian pianist and composer.

On 19 January Haydn was granted the highest honour of being invited to the Royal Court Ball on the Queen's birthday. Here he was warmly greeted by the Prince of Wales, the future King George IV. The following day he went to the Prince's residence, Carlton House, where he took part in a musical evening. This was the first of a number of visits to Carlton House where he enjoyed the company, the music and the food.

Music in London at the time of Haydn's arrival was flourishing; England was certainly not a 'Land Without Music' at the end of the eighteenth century. The Academy of Ancient Music, established in 1710, consisting of about 65 players and singers, gave regular concerts which were well attended; their first violinist was none other than Salomon himself. The rival Professional Concerts were likewise well patronised. In addition, the numerous choral and instrumental societies frequently promoted performances so that the capital was not lacking in musical activities.

Through contractual difficulties, Salomon's concerts were postponed several times. The first of them in which Haydn eventually participated took place on 11 March in the Hanover Square Rooms. The programme opened with an Overture by Rosetti, and included a group of songs and arias, an oboe concerto, a violin concerto and a concertante for 'pedal harp' and piano played by Madame Krumpholtz and Jan Ladislav Dussek.

Haydn's contribution, his first work for an English audience, was in the custom of the day described on the programme as

'A New Grand Overture': it was in fact the Symphony known today as No. 96 in D, at one time called the *Miracle*, a title now rightly transferred to Symphony No. 102 in B flat.* The considerable success of this concert at once dispelled the malicious rumours spread by Salomon's enemies that Haydn was now an old man whose powers were declining. Haydn himself directed the performance from the harpsichord while Salomon led the orchestra. The band, at around forty strong but with no clarinets, was about twice the size of that at Esterháza and the standard of playing much impressed the composer.

The next morning, the *Morning Chronicle* published the following report:

SALOMON'S CONCERT

The First Concert under the auspices of HAYDN was last night, and never, perhaps, was there a richer musical treat. It is not wonderful that to souls capable of being touched by music, HAYDN should be an object of homage and even of idolatry; for like our own SHAKSPEARE [*sic*], he moves and governs the passions at his will. His new Grand Overture was pronounced by every scientific ear to be a most wonderful composition; but the first movement in particular rises in grandeur of subject, and in the rich variety of *air* and passion, beyond any even of his own productions. The *Overture* has four movements—An Allegro —Andante—Minuet—and Rondo. They are all beautiful, but the first is pre-eminent in every charm and the Band performed it with admirable correctness. . . . We were happy to see the Concert so well attended the first night; for we cannot suppress our very anxious hopes, that the first musical genius of the age may be induced, by our liberal welcome, to take up his residence in England.

One of those present at this concert was Dr. Charles Burney, then organist at Chelsea Hospital, who wrote:

Haydn himself presided at the pianoforte [*sic*]: and the sight of that renowned composer so electrified the audience, as to excite an attention and pleasure superior to any that had ever, to my knowledge, been caused by instrumental music in England. The slow movement was encored; which never before happened, I believe, in any country.

This was probably the first time that Haydn had witnessed the

* After the first performance of the Symphony in B flat in February 1795, the audience pressed to the front of the hall in their enthusiasm. At that moment a huge chandelier fell from the ceiling into the space where the audience had earlier been seated. The fact that no one was hurt was deemed a 'miracle'.

pleasure and enthusiasm of an audience who had paid to attend a concert. The reception of his music and the favourable newspaper reports must have delighted him greatly.

All the concerts of the planned series were greeted with the same rapturous applause. At the final benefit concert on 16 May (three more followed, closing the season on 3 June), Haydn received more than £350, well in excess of the £200 sum previously guaranteed by Salomon. This visit to London marked a new burst of creative activity in the composer. Away from the restrictions of Esterháza and the burden of administrative work which must have wasted so much of his time there, Haydn discovered a freedom and confidence which produced his finest symphonies.

In the meantime he had been asked to write an opera, and he chose a version of the Orpheus story, *L'anima del filosofo* (*The Soul of the Philosopher*), based on a libretto by Badini. When it was completed, however, Sir John Gallini, the impressario, was unable to produce it through the intrigues of his rivals at the Italian Opera House in the Pantheon. This company had the patronage of the King so that they managed to prevent Gallini from obtaining a licence to perform operas. Although the project was abandoned, Haydn was paid in full for the completed work. After this, he seems to have lost interest in the opera which was never performed elsewhere. Gallini lost over £2,000 on the enterprise.

In May 1791, a Handel Festival was mounted in Westminster Abbey on a huge scale, with over a thousand singers and players. This was probably the beginning of the English tradition for performing Handel's oratorios with vast forces. Haydn attended these concerts and the experience had an enormous effect upon him. He had never heard music performed in such a way and may not have been familiar with Handel's choral masterpieces. After one performance of *Messiah* and of the 'Hallelujah' chorus in particular, he said of Handel, 'He is the master of us all.' It was as a direct result of this festival that Haydn began to consider the possibility of composing an oratorio himself.

After another choral concert, this time in St. Paul's Cathedral in the following year, he wrote in his diary, 'No music has ever moved me so much in my life as this devout and innocent one.'

In July 1791, Haydn was invited to Oxford in order to receive an honorary Doctorate of Music. It was Dr. Charles Burney who had recommended the composer for this award. Haydn submitted his Symphony No. 92 in G, written originally for Paris but now universally known as the *Oxford*. He also composed a three-part canon *Thy Voice, O Harmony, is divine* as his exercise.

Dr. Charles Burney (1726–1814). Portrait by Reynolds (British Museum)

The Italian Opera House

The only feature of the ceremony on 8 July which gave the composer dismay was the cost. Ever careful over his own expenses, he was displeased at having to pay one and a half guineas for the ringing of the bells, another half guinea for the hire of the robes and six guineas for the journey. He was, however, very proud of the honour bestowed upon him. 'I only wish my Viennese friends could have seen me', he wrote in a letter. Three concerts were given in Oxford as part of the celebrations for the composer. One of the soloists at the second concert was the young violinist, Franz Clement, then only eleven years old, for whom Beethoven was to compose his Violin Concerto in 1806.

Although Haydn made no reference to the architecture of Oxford, he made notes in his diary of his impressions of Cambridge which he visited shortly afterwards:

Westminster Abbey and
St. Margaret's Church,
1793

The Hall and Chapel,
Oriel College, Oxford

Each university [college] has at the back of it a very spacious and
beautiful garden, with stone bridges in order to afford a crossing over
the river which winds past. King's College Chapel is famous for its
carvings. It is all stone and so delicate that nothing more beautiful
could have been made in wood. It has already endured four hundred

years,* yet everyone would think its age about ten years because of the firmness and peculiar whiteness of the stone.

* Haydn is not quite accurate. King's College Chapel was begun in 1446 and completed in 1515.

The South Side of
King's College Chapel,
Cambridge

The Quadrangle of
Trinity College,
Cambridge

For Haydn, a man who had been tied to the Esterházy household for almost thirty years, the freedom to go where he pleased
without first having to beg permission, was itself most gratifying.
In early August he went with a boating party down the Thames
from Westminster Bridge to Richmond where they had a picnic
on an island. They were accompanied on the water by another
boat containing a wind band. After this he went to stay with the
family of a London banker, Mr. Brassey, in the countryside of
Hertfordshire, twelve miles outside London. It was here that he
composed the two symphonies, No. 93 in D and No. 94 in G, the
Surprise. To Marianne von Genzinger he wrote:

For the last two months [actually only five weeks] I have been
living in the country, amid the loveliest scenery, with the family of a
banker where the atmosphere is like that of the Genzinger household,
and where I live as though I were in a monastery. I am working hard;
each morning I walk in the woods with my English grammar. I think
of my Creator, and all my friends I have left behind. How sweet this
liberty really is.

The Prince of Wales
after he became king.
Portrait by Thomas
Lawrence (Vatican Art
Gallery, Rome)

94

Back in the capital at the end of that month, Haydn still found time for composition as the concert season had not begun. He continued to pay visits to places of interest in and around London. On 5 November, he was entertained to dinner by the Lord Mayor; in his diary he complains of the poor quality of the music provided for dancing.

On 25 November he was an honoured guest for a few days at Oatlands, the country mansion in Surrey where the Duke of York was spending his honeymoon. The new bride, the seventeen-year old daughter of King Friedrich Wilhelm II of Prussia was well acquainted with many of Haydn's works, and was one of his most ardent admirers. The Prince of Wales (later George IV) joined in the musical gatherings and performed 'very tolerably' on the cello.

The Prince of Wales commissioned John Hoppner to paint a portrait of Haydn. When the composer sat in a chair posing for the artist, his usually jovial expression changed to one of uncharacteristic seriousness. In order to restore his true expression, it was arranged that a German chamber maid should be employed to engage the composer in conversation during the sitting. The result is the portrait, now in the collection at Buckingham Palace, showing Haydn in a relaxed mood.

It was at this time that Haydn received the shattering news of the death of Mozart. To Marianne von Genzinger he wrote:

I shall be sorry when I come back to Vienna to feel the loss of Mozart. More than a century will pass before a talent such as his will be found again.

Haydn continued to be a popular guest among the nobility in London; the ladies in particular seemed to have been attracted to him. His genial personality and subtle flattery ensured their friendships. He was on close terms with many of them but with one in particular, Mrs. Rebecca Schroter, the widow of a musician, he seems to have been very friendly. To Albert Christoph Dies he confided that if he had been single at the time he would have married her.

She wrote many affectionate love letters to him which he carefully copied into his diary. Haydn still wrote frequently to two other women for whom he had strong feelings, Luigia Polzelli, the singer from Esterháza who was then living in Italy, and Marianne von Genzinger.

Another friend of the composer was John Hunter, a famous surgeon, and his wife Anne who wrote the verses for Haydn's *Six Original Canzonettas*. Hunter offered to remove a polypus which

Haydn. Portrait by John Hoppner, 1792 (Buckingham Palace, reproduced by gracious permission of Her Majesty the Queen)

St. Paul's Cathedral.
Engraving by J. Tingle
after the drawing by
T. H. Shepherd

Haydn had in his nose from which he had suffered much of his life. When Haydn arrived at Hunter's surgery he was alarmed to see four sturdy men who were to hold him down during the operation. Taking fright at this, he shouted and struggled so much that any attempt to operate had to be abandoned.

The petty rivalries amongst concert promoters in London continued to plague the composer. The organisers of the Professional Concerts, for instance, spread malicious rumours that he was no longer capable of composing good music on account of his advancing age. They also engaged the services of the young Ignaz Pleyel, from Strassburg, who had been a pupil of Haydn at Esterháza. Although Pleyel is remembered now only as the writer of instructional music for the violin and a maker of pianos and harps, he was at this time acquiring a reputation as a composer of great promise.

The conflict between the followers of Haydn and those of Pleyel resembles the feuds between the supporters of Brahms and Wagner in Germany over half a century later. It is to the credit of both Haydn and Pleyel that although they were acutely aware of the situation they remained the best of friends, continuing to meet frequently and even attending each other's concerts: Haydn

Ignaz Pleyel (1757–
1831). Engraving by
J. Neidl after the
painting by Thomas
Hardy, 1793

indeed was the conspicuous guest at Pleyel's first Professional Concert on 13 February 1792, when the programme included symphonies by Haydn himself as well as Mozart and Pleyel.

In spite of this friendship, each composer still felt the necessity to vindicate his own reputation with the result that they were forced into composing new music for every concert. For Haydn, who had never been a fast worker, this proved a great strain ('Never in all my life have I written so much in one year as I did in the past twelve months'). Nevertheless, each concert of this second season was a triumph, with the critics unanimously echoing the enthusiasm of the audiences in their praise of every new work.

When the season was over, Haydn was worn out through

Over page

Ascot Heath Races: 'In the first heat,' wrote Haydn, 'there were three riders who where compelled to go around the course twice without stopping. They did it in five minutes. No stranger would believe it unless he were convinced by observation. The second time there were seven riders and when they approached some fell back, but never more than about ten paces and when one thinks the one rider who is about to reach the goal will be the first, at which moment large bets are laid on him, another rushes past him with inconceivable force and reaches the winning post. The riders are very lightly clad in silk, each of a different colour, to make it easier to recognise them and all lean as greyhounds. The

horses are of the finest breeds, light, with very slender legs, the manes plaited into braids, the hoofs very neat. As soon as they hear the sound of the bell they dash off with the greatest force. Every leap of the horses is twenty-two feet long. These horses are very costly. A few years ago the Prince of Wales paid eight thousand pounds for one and sold it again for six thousand. But the first time he won fifty thousand pounds with it. I saw eight heats the first day, and in spite of a heavy rain there were two thousand vehicles, all full of people, and three times as many people were present on foot. Besides this there are all kinds of puppet plays, *ciarlatanz* [sic], conjurors, and buffoons performing during the races, and in a multitude of tents food and all kinds of wine and beer . . .' (14 June 1792)

Bonn, a general view.
Coloured engraving by
J. Ziegler after
L. Janscha

composing and his frequent appearances in public. He had also spent much of his time and energy on giving music lessons and writing various short pieces of music to satisfy the demands of publishers. Among these items were arrangements of Scottish folk-songs which he had made for William Napier, a Scottish violinist who had turned to being a music publisher through ill health. Haydn wished to help him earn a living and the joint project brought wide recognition to both composer and publisher.

Towards the end and after the second season of concerts in London in the early summer of 1792, Haydn again took every opportunity of visiting places of interest. On 22 May he went to Ranelagh Gardens which he considered a place without equal in the whole world. Considering the magnificence of Esterháza, this was indeed a great tribute. Later, he much admired St. George's Chapel at Windsor, but he was more intrigued by an excursion to the races at Ascot, which he made on 14 June. The next day at

Slough, he met William Herschel, the German musician and amateur astronomer who had discovered the planet Uranus in 1781.

By the mid-summer of 1792, Haydn felt the need to end his long stay in England, partly as he had again been requested by Prince Esterházy to return, and partly in order to see to his business affairs in Vienna. His London leave-taking was as sad an occasion as his departure from Vienna eighteen months previously. He had made so many friends that he was naturally reluctant to go. However he gave assurances that he would return to London as soon as he was able.

On his journey to Vienna, he again stopped in Bonn, and it is widely accepted that it was on the occasion of this visit that the twenty-one year old Beethoven showed him a cantata he had composed which so impressed the master that he offered to give the young man lessons in composition. It was in Bonn, too, that he met Simrock, the publisher. By the last week of July he had reached Vienna.

Chapter 12

The Grand Mogul

'Labour assiduously and receive Mozart's spirit from the hands of Haydn'—Count Waldstein

After the excitement and activity of London, Vienna was by comparison a dull city for Haydn. In contrast to his reception in England, his arrival in the Austrian capital passed unnoticed. Naturally he was much welcomed by his numerous friends, but no concerts were given in his honour, nor did the newspapers report his return.

In August 1793 on the insistence of his wife, he bought a house in Vienna, but he made certain that she never lived there herself. In the same year, his friend Marianne von Genzinger died suddenly at the age of thirty-eight. Her death had a profound effect upon the composer as he thereby lost the one remaining person to whom he could speak with complete frankness and whose confidence he trusted. With an almost complete estrangement between himself and his wife, he was now a lonely old man.

In the meantime, during the late autumn of 1792, Beethoven arrived in Vienna in order to receive instruction in composition from Haydn. Unfortunately the differing temperaments of the two men prevented the growth of any close friendship; Mozart and Haydn had also possessed seemingly conflicting characteristics but their enormous respect for each other brought about a remarkable relationship instead.

Haydn was now sixty, Beethoven twenty-two, but their lack of rapport cannot be attributed to the gulf in years which separated them. Beethoven was a born rebel, unprepared to compromise, or to subdue his own erratic moods, totally lacking in modesty and naturally distrustful of so respected a man as Haydn.

As Beethoven had so little money, Haydn charged him only eight groschen (about a shilling) for each lesson. In the summer of 1793, he took his pupil to Eisenstadt and at first considered inviting him to go on the second visit to England. But Haydn realised that the ungrateful young man would be a poor companion and decided against such a proposal. To Beethoven,

Vienna seen from the Belvedere, 1759–61. Painting by Bernardo Bellotto (Vienna, Kunsthistorisches Museum). In the centre is the Schwarzenberg Palace, the scene of Haydn's last triumphs

Beethoven's sketches for the finale of his Piano Trio in C minor, Op. 1, No. 3, published in 1795. According to a contemporary, Ferdinand Ries, Haydn 'advised Beethoven not to publish the third [trio] in C minor. This astonished Beethoven, inasmuch as he considered the third the best of the Trios . . . Consequently Haydn's remark left a bad impression on Beethoven and led him to think that Haydn was envious, jealous and ill-disposed towards him' (British Museum, Kafka Sketchbook)

Haydn once remarked: 'You give me the impression of being a man who has several heads, several hearts and several souls'.

Beethoven wished to be instructed in strict counterpoint, but Haydn could summon little interest in such academic exercises. For this reason the dissatisfied young man secretly sought tuition from Johann Schenk, a composer and music teacher. Some years later, Haydn discovered the duplicity of his pupil, but still remained on relatively friendly terms with him.

Haydn often took great pains to assist Beethoven, but was sadly disillusioned several times to learn of his pupil's deceit. On 23 November 1793, Haydn wrote to the Elector of Bonn requesting that Beethoven's allowance for studying in Vienna should be increased. To support his plea, he made reference to a number of fine compositions which the young man had written under his guidance. In the letter, Haydn stated prophetically, 'Beethoven will eventually attain the position of one of the greatest composer's in Europe, and I shall be proud to call myself his teacher'.

To his dismay, Haydn received a letter from the Elector refusing to increase the allowance, and stating that all the works of Beethoven mentioned by Haydn with one exception had been composed before he left Bonn for Vienna. Beethoven foolishly thought that jealousy motivated his teacher's criticism of his music. Clearly Haydn's selfless attitude towards the genius of Mozart shows that Beethoven had a totally wrong conception of Haydn's motives.

As he grew older and more experienced, Beethoven gradually realised the true nature of Haydn the man, and in March 1808 was present at a performance of *The Creation* to pay tribute to the aged composer on his last appearance in Vienna.

Chapter 13
London: 1794–95

'This ever righteous and greatly respected man'—Count Chotek

By the summer of 1793, Haydn had planned a second visit to London. He had found life in Vienna little compensation for the constantly stimulating activity of England. After obtaining with some difficulty the permission of Prince Esterházy, Haydn set out on 19 January of the following year, taking with him his servant and copyist, Johann Elssler (junior).

London, the Tower, 1821

The two men arrived in London on 4 February where Haydn

had to prepare immediately for the first concert which took place on 10 February. Once again the audience received the great man with enthusiasm. For this first series of concerts under Salomon's direction, he provided three symphonies: No. 99 in E flat, No. 100 in G (the *Military*) and No. 101 in D (the *Clock*).

It was also in London in 1794 that Haydn made his first attempt at composing an oratorio using Handel as his model. As a text he chose a poem by Marchmont Nedham entitled *Invocation to Neptune for the Commonwealth of England*. After completing only a bass aria and a chorus, he abandoned the project as he felt that his command of English was not good enough. The manuscript of this music is now in the British Museum.

Haydn was delighted to renew the friendships he had made on his first visit, and he also became acquainted with other important musicians of the day, including the violinist Viotti, Domenico Dragonetti, the double-bass virtuoso, and the English composer, William Shield, whose opera *The Woodman* Haydn had heard at Covent Garden in 1791.

In the meantime his customary care over performances and preparation was frequently in evidence. On one occasion while rehearsing, for example, Haydn impressed the orchestral players by showing the inexperienced timpani player how he wanted the drum sticks to be handled. It should be remembered that Haydn himself as a boy of only six had learnt to play the drums when he was in Hainburg. Two members of Salomon's London orchestra later emigrated to the United States where they soon became established as important musicians. James Hewitt (1770–1827), an exact contemporary of Beethoven, played the violin under Haydn in 1791. He went to America in 1792. He settled in New York and became a leading figure in concert promotion. He was responsible for the first performance of many of Haydn's works in the New World, including the première in New York of the *Seven Last Words* given on 25 March 1793.

The other musician was Johann Christian Gottlieb Graupner (1767–1836) of German birth, who was an oboist under Haydn in London. Some time during the 1790s he went to America, settling first in South Carolina but later moving to Boston. In 1810 he founded the Philharmonic Society of Boston for the express purpose of practising Haydn's symphonies. In 1815 he helped to organise the first Handel and Haydn Society to perform the great sacred choral masterpieces by these two composers and generally to improve the standard of choral singing throughout New England.

Haydn again took every opportunity to visit notable places throughout the South of England. He went to Hampton Court

Haydn. Pencil sketch by George Dance, London 20 March 1794

Hampton Court Palace,
1827

Symphony No. 102.
Autograph (Tübingen,
Universitätsbibliothek)

and Winchester. Later he crossed the Solent to Cowes in the Isle of Wight and admired the view from Carisbrooke Castle. In August 1794 he stayed for three days at Bath which he declared to be one of the most beautiful towns in the whole of Europe. Here he was entertained with lavish hospitality by a local musician of Italian origin, Venanzio Rauzzini.

By way of Bristol, he travelled back to London, where he made preparations for a second season of concerts. These were organised by the Opera Concerts (under the direction of Viotti and not Salomon who in the January of 1795 announced the end of his famous series of concerts) and took place in the King's Theatre in Haymarket. The orchestra for these occasions comprised over sixty players, including around 24 violins, and four each of flutes, oboes, clarinets and bassoons. For the eleven concerts (given between 2 February and 1 June), Haydn composed a number of works including his last three symphonies: No. 102 in

B flat, now known as the *Miracle*, No. 103 in E flat (the *Drum Roll*) and No. 104 in D (the *London*).

At a special concert given on 7 February in York House by the Duke of York, Haydn was presented to King George III. As usual, Haydn directed the performance from the keyboard and

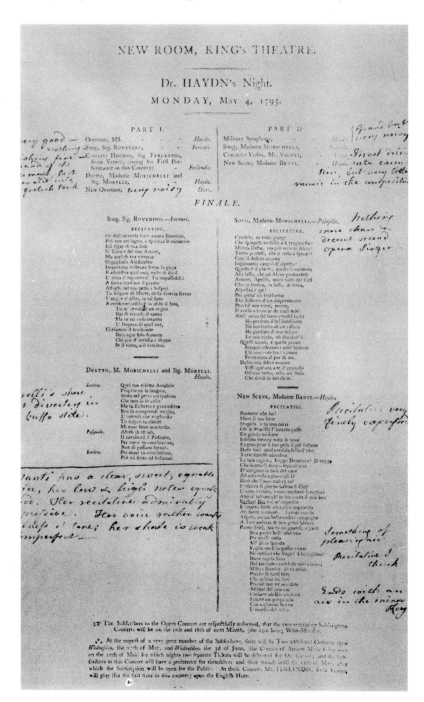

Handbill for Haydn's Benefit Concert, King's Theatre, 4 May 1795 (Albi Rosenthal Collection)

afterwards entertained the company with songs and keyboard pieces. This was the first of many musical evenings that Haydn attended in the company of members of the Royal family. Once again Haydn was urged by them to make his home permanently in England. It is probable that he considered the proposal seriously, especially as the months in Vienna after his first London visit had not been particularly happy for him.

Living in London was certainly rewarding for him both musically and financially, but the arduous activities were beginning to fatigue the sixty-three year old composer. He was perhaps hoping to settle down to a less exacting routine.

On the death of Prince Anton Esterházy in 1794, his successor, Nicholas II, grandson of Nicholas I, wrote to Haydn asking him to return to Eisenstadt as he was intending to reconstitute the orchestra and choir his father had disbanded. The palace at

King's Theatre, Haymarket, after rebuilding. Drawing by R. B. Schnebbelie, 1820 (British Museum, Crace Collection)

Esterháza had been abandoned in 1791, and except for the celebrations in August of that year when Prince Anton had been installed as lord-lieutenant of the province, the place had remained unused. By 1803 the puppet theatre at Esterháza had become a store for hunting equipment. The beautiful theatre was stacked full of straw and in 1832 was turned into a timber store-shed. By 1900 only indistinct traces of ruins remained of the once magnificent palace of Esterháza.

The Esterházy household had returned to the castle at Eisenstadt. Haydn was still officially director of music to the Prince, but Joseph Weigl, once a cellist in Haydn's orchestra there, and at that time conductor of the Imperial Court Theatre in Vienna, had taken Haydn's place while he was in London on the few occasions that music was required.

After a final series of concerts in May and June, 1795, Haydn was eventually able to say farewell to his many friends in London. He left England on 15 August, armed with numerous presents from his well-wishers, the scores of many new works he had composed during the previous eighteen months and almost £1,200 he had earned through his compositions and concerts.

Chapter 14

Vienna—the mature years

'And the Spirit of God moved upon the face of the waters'—*Genesis* I:2

On his return journey, Haydn went out of his way to visit Hamburg where he hoped to meet C. P. E. Bach whose keyboard works he had admired as a young man. To his deep regret, he learnt that Bach had died seven years earlier in 1788.

From Hamburg, he travelled to Frankfurt where Prince Esterházy was attending the coronation of the Emperor Franz II. From there the Prince and Haydn returned together to Vienna.

Haydn went back into service with the Esterházy family with certain misgivings. Although possessing an interest in music, Prince Nicholas II much preferred old-fashioned Austrian church music. The personal relationship between the prince and the composer was strained since the former did little to disguise his haughty distaste for Haydn's compositions. Haydn must have frequently looked back with nostalgia to his visits to England, where his talents had been so widely appreciated. Now at Eisenstadt he was often in conflict with his patron and burdened with the administrative routine which consumed precious time that could have been devoted to composition.

In deference to the Prince's taste, Haydn composed six large-scale settings of the Mass, a second *Te Deum* in C and the two crowning masterpieces of his whole career, *The Creation* and *The Seasons*.

The first of these Masses composed in 1796 is in C major; it acquired the title *Missa in Tempore Belli* (*Mass in time of war*) as it was written while Napoleon was invading northern Italy on his way towards the Austrian frontier. Haydn made use of trumpets and drums especially in the *Agnus Dei*, which calls to mind the feeling of war. The Mass was first performed at Eisenstadt on 13 September in honour of Princess Maria Josepha Ermenegild, wife of Prince Nicholas.

The second Mass in B flat was also composed in 1796. It was given the subtitle *Heiligmesse* from the hymn tune *Heilig, heilig* which is interpolated into the *Sanctus*. In 1798, during the composition of the third Mass in D minor, news came to Haydn that Nelson had won the Battle of the Nile. From this association, the Mass is often called the *Nelson*, but it is also known as the *Imperial*. The orchestration, unusually, omits all woodwind instruments, the work being scored for three trumpets, timpani and strings. The use of trumpets in the *Benedictus* is generally assumed to be a symbolic representation of Nelson's victory at the Battle of the Nile.

The fourth Mass, also in B flat and known as the *Maria Theresa*, was composed in 1799. The fifth Mass, again in B flat and written in 1801, was given the title *Creation Mass* as a theme from the oratorio appears in the *Agnus Dei*.

The sixth Mass, yet again in B flat and composed in 1802, was

The *Nelson* or *Imperial* Mass. Autograph page from the 'Kyrie' (Vienna, National-bibliothek)

The Creation. Autograph sketches for the first aria of Gabriel (*ibid*)

Haydn's last important work. It is known as the *Harmonie Messe* on account of the extensive use of wind instruments ('Harmonie' is the German word for a band of wind instruments).

All these Masses employ four soloists who sing for the most part as an ensemble with only short passages for the individual voices. In this respect, they perhaps had an influence upon Beethoven's three important masterpieces, the two Masses and the *Choral Symphony*, where the vocal quartet also sing much of the time as a group.

The closing years of Haydn's composing career reached their climax in the two great choral works *The Creation* and *The Seasons*. The performance of *Messiah* in Westminster Abbey in 1791 as part of the Handel Festival had convinced Haydn that he must compose a large-scale oratorio. He had earlier completed an oratorio in the Italian style, *The Return of Tobias* in 1775, but his proposed new work was intended to be on the scale of Handel's *Messiah*.

Haydn's choice of subject and text of *The Creation* may have been made in London where it is believed he was shown the libretto of an oratorio based on Milton's *Paradise Lost* which had been compiled for Handel but never set by him. Haydn may have taken this libretto back to Vienna where it was translated into German by Baron Gottfried van Swieten, an Austrian diplomat

Baron Gottfried van Swieten (1733–1803)

Vienna, the National-bibliothek on the Josephplatz. Coloured engraving by Schütz, 1780. It was in this building that the Baron van Swieten had a flat where he was regularly visited by both Mozart and Haydn, and, later, Beethoven

and Court Librarian. Van Swieten was a keen music lover who possessed a particular admiration for the works of Handel. It was he who asked Mozart to provide wind parts for *Messiah* for a performance where no organ was available. This version with a few alterations is still the basic one used today on most occasions.

Van Swieten not only translated the words of *The Creation* but also provided a guarantee to the composer against the cost of the eventual performance. Haydn began the work early in 1796 taking two years to complete it. Although he was now in his mid-sixties and devoted considerable time and energy to the oratorio, he found the task less fatiguing and more satisfying than anything else he had written before. His personal religious feelings were strongly stimulated:

Never before was I so devout as when I composed *The Creation*. I knelt down each day to pray to God to give me strength for my work.

This oratorio was Haydn's first religious choral work using German instead of Latin words, and the first performance was given on 29 April 1798 to a private audience of the nobility in the

Covent Garden Theatre as seen by Thomas Rowlandson, *c.* 1810 (John Brook)

Schwarzenberg Palace in Vienna. The occasion aroused an enthusiasm similar to the composer's reception in London. Large crowds who were unable to enter the palace gathered outside to share in the excitement. Haydn conducted the performance with an orchestra of over 180 players. The audience, not familiar with the huge scale Handel Festivals in England, found the experience overwhelming. After so many years Haydn at last witnessed a triumph in his own city of Vienna.

The Creation was repeated the following day and again on 7 and 8 May, each time at the Schwarzenberg Palace. From these and a number of subsequent performances Haydn received a considerable sum of money. The first public hearing of the work took place on 19 March 1799 in the Vienna Kärntnertor theatre.

The London première of the oratorio was given on 28 March 1800 in Covent Garden Theatre, directed by John Ashley, a

123

rival of Salomon. The latter had hoped to secure the first performance but his score of the work did not arrive in time from Vienna. The Salomon concert took place in the King's Theatre, Haymarket on 21 April. In the same year is was performed at the Three Choirs Festival at Worcester, and repeated at Hereford in 1801 and Gloucester in 1802.

Haydn was invited to Paris for the first performance there of *The Creation*, but with the state of war between Austria and France he could not undertake such a visit. In addition, the health of the sixty-eight year old composer would not have

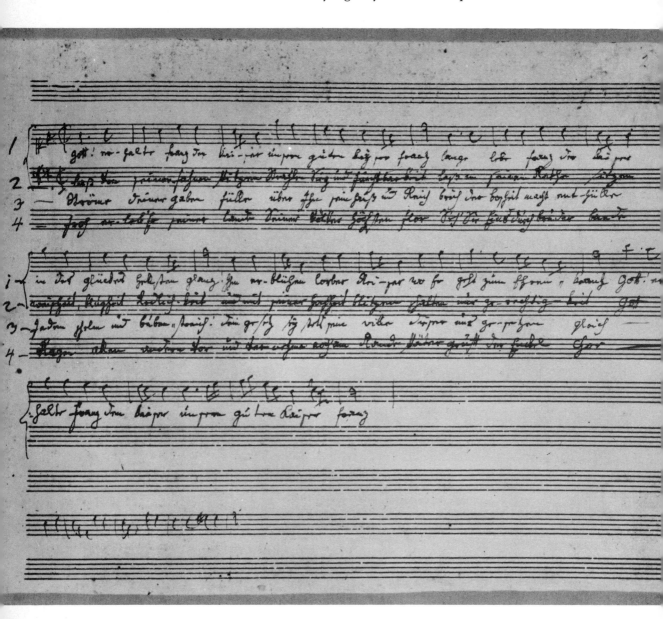

withstood the journey. The Paris concert, which had been sold out fifteen days before, was held on 24 December 1800. The great success of the occasion was overshadowed by an attempted assassination by bomb on the life of Napoleon who was on his way to attend the concert.

While writing *The Creation*, Haydn composed several other works. In 1796 he wrote a Concerto in E flat for keyed trumpet, which has proved to be the most popular of all his concertos and the best known in the trumpet repertoire. It was also the first piece to be composed for a trumpet with keys to enable the performer to play chromatically outside the open notes of the natural trumpet.* Although the precise instrument for which the concerto was written is not known, it is probable that it had a number of holes in the tube which could be opened and closed by means of keys. This system proved cumbersome and detrimental both to tone and intonation so that it was later abandoned in favour of valves which were incorporated into the trumpet during the first decade of the nineteenth century. It is surprising, incidentally, to discover that the Trumpet Concerto disappeared from the concert hall soon after Haydn's death and did not re-emerge again until 1928 when it was broadcast by George Eskdale who later recorded the second and third movements. This brilliant work admirably suits the character of the trumpet and is still the finest concerto for the instrument.

During the same year, Haydn composed his last work for the stage. He provided incidental music for a play *The Patriot King, or Alfred and Elvida* by the English playwright Alexander Bicknell. For a production in a German translation in Vienna, he wrote a recitative, aria and chorus.

While in England, Haydn had been impressed by the playing of *God Save the King*. In Vienna he felt that the Austrian people, who were suffering from low morale through the lack of success in the war against Napoleon, would benefit from the adoption of a patriotic hymn as a national anthem. In January 1797, he accordingly set a short text by Leopold Haschka for this purpose. This anthem *Gotte erhalte Franz den Kaiser (God Save the Emperor Franz)* was at once adopted by the people and in the event remained the official Austrian National Anthem for over a century. On 12 February the Emperor's birthday, copies of the words and music were distributed at the Burgtheater in Vienna. At the entry of the Emperor, the whole audience rose and sang the hymn. On the same evening it was given before the performance in every theatre throughout the city. In gratitude, the Emperor presented a gold snuff box to Haydn.

The *Kaiserhymne*.
Autograph (Vienna,
Nationalbibliothek)

* *cf* comments on the horn, p. 50.

Autograph of the opening of Haydn's last Piano Sonata, composed in London in 1794 and published by Artaria in Vienna in December 1798. Haydn wrote over sixty sonatas for keyboard (Washington, Library of Congress)

Chapter 15

The Final Decade

'Gone is all my strength, old and weak am I'—Haydn after Gellert

A document in the Salzburg Mozarteum throws considerable light upon Haydn's daily routine. It is probable that this description was written by Johann Elssler, his copyist and general assistant.

In the summer, he always rose at 6.30 am. His first task was to shave, which he did himself until he was seventy-three. After shaving he completed dressing. If a pupil had arrived, he made him play his piece while the composer dressed. Mistakes were promptly corrected and a new piece for practising was given to him. Perhaps an hour and a half would be spent in this way. Precisely at 8.0 o'clock, breakfast was taken. Immediately afterwards, he would sit at the piano and improvise, making sketches of compositions until 11.30 am. Then he received visitors or paid calls or went for a walk until 1.30 pm. Between 2.0 and 3.0 pm he dined, after which he either attended to domestic matters or returned to his music. Then he took the sketches he had made in the morning and scored them. In the evening at 8.0 pm he would go out, returning home at 9.0 pm to orchestrate or read a book until 10.0 o'clock. At 10 he had a supper of bread and wine; he made it a rule never to eat an evening meal of anything but bread and wine, except when he was invited out. At half past eleven he went to bed, in old age even later. In winter his routine did not vary much except that he got up half-an-hour later. In his last five or six years, old age and illness upset this timetable.

In the early spring of 1800, Haydn sent his wife to Baden to take the spa waters. At Baden in March, at the age of seventy, she died of arthritis.

After further performances of *The Creation* in Vienna at the Tokunstler Societat on 15 March and at the Schwarzenberg Palace on 12 and 13 April, Haydn went back to Eisenstadt, where he spent the summer busily engaged on the second oratorio *The Seasons*.

In September 1800, Eisenstadt received a group of distinguished travellers from abroad. Admiral Nelson with Sir William and

Haydn. Medallion by
N. Gatteaux, Paris 1800

Lady Hamilton was returning to England from Naples where Sir William had been Ambassador. After three weeks in Vienna, the party set out in the evening of Saturday, 6 September for Eisenstadt.

The Prince and Princess Esterházy had previously visited the Naples Court and Haydn had met the Hamiltons during his second stay in London. Indeed Sir William was one of the subscribers to a collection of Scottish folk songs which Haydn had arranged for Thomson, the Edinburgh publisher.

The day after their arrival, the visitors were treated to a display of fireworks, followed on Monday, 8 September, by a ball and on Tuesday by a hunting party. It is said that Lady Hamilton hardly left the composer's side during the whole of her time at Eisenstadt. Haydn sent off to Vienna for a copy of his solo cantata *Ariadne on Naxos* (1789) which Lady Hamilton later sang to his accompaniment. They also performed a special 'Nelson' aria, *Lines from the Battle of the Nile*. The words for this were written by Lady Hamilton's companion, Mrs. Cornelia Knight.

During their stay, the English party attended a performance of a new Mass composed by Haydn; it is unlikely that this was the Mass in D minor, later known as the *Nelson* Mass, but it may have been the so-called *Creation* Mass in B flat. On each of the four evenings, there were concerts given by the chorus and orchestra. There appears to be no truth, by the way, in a widely current story of the time that Nelson asked Haydn for his pen, in return presenting his gold watch to the composer. The fact that Haydn shortly afterwards gave a gold watch to his brother Michael as compensation for one stolen from him by French soldiers looting in Salzburg, and that in addition, when Haydn died, two portraits of Nelson and a chart of the Battle of the Nile were found amongst his possession, seems insubstantial evidence to support such a story—coincidences can perhaps be taken too far, just as can the friendship of the two men.

For the secular oratorio *The Seasons*, van Swieten translated and adapted a poem of the same name by the Scottish poet James Thomson (1700–1748) whose best-known work was 'Rule Britannia' from his masque *Alfred* (set to music by Thomas Arne in 1740). The poem portrays the changing countryside during the year. Haydn's music illustrates many features of nature including bird song, thunder and even the croaking of a frog.

The first performance of Haydn's new work took place in Prince Schwarzenberg's Palace on 24 April 1801. In May, two performances were given at court where the Empress Maria Theresia sang the soprano solos. The first public concert produc-

Lady Emma Hamilton (1765–1815). Portrait by G. Romney (London, National Portrait Gallery)

130

The Seasons. Autograph sketches for part of the fourth section, 'Winter' (Tübingen, Universitätsbibliothek)

Admiral Lord Nelson (1758–1805). Portrait by Hoppner, 1801 (London, St. James Palace)

tion of *The Seasons* took place in the same month at the Redoutensaal Theatre in Vienna.

As with *The Creation*, every presentation of *The Seasons* was greeted with great excitement and appreciation by large audiences. Once more Haydn earned a large sum of money with the work, but the writing of it had left him totally exhausted. In 1805 he said: '*The Seasons* did not bring me luck. I should not have written it. It has worn me out'.

Haydn now felt his strength waning and in 1801 he decided to make his will. Only the meeting with his brothers Michael and Johann Evangelist in September brought him any happiness at this time. In the following year he conceived the plan for another large scale oratorio on the subject of the Last Judgement, but the death of van Swieten in 1802 may have been the reason he did not pursue the project.

His last two works date from 1802 and 1803, the *Harmonie*

131

I. F. REICHARDT.

Tonkünstler und Schriftsteller.

132

Mass and his incomplete quartet Op. 103 in B flat, which was published in its two movement form in 1806. He also finished a further set of Scottish folk-song arrangements for William Whyte, an Edinburgh publisher, who paid 500 florins for them. Of these pieces, he said: 'I boast of this work and by it I flatter myself my name will live in Scotland many years after my death'.

During Haydn's final years, numerous honours came to him from all over Europe. He took great pride in the medals and gifts which had been presented to him, and often showed them to his visitors. When J. F. Reichardt, who had been *Kapellmeister* to Frederick the Great of Prussia, visited Haydn in November 1808, the composer showed him the black ebony box presented to him by Princess Esterházy. On the lid of this box was painted the scene at the University Great Hall during the performance of *The Creation* on 27 March of that year.* Reichardt also saw gold medals from Russia and Paris, a magnificent ring sent to the composer by the Czar of Russia, and numerous diplomas from almost every city in Europe, including the freedom of Vienna, which was granted him in 1804. Reichardt said, 'In these things, the kindly old man seems to live his life happily all over again'.

In his letters and conversations, Haydn frequently made reference to his failing strength and weakening mental ability. To a man who had hardly experienced any sickness during his life, the gradual deterioration in his health caused him great anguish. He had printed for his use a visiting card which he sent to people in reply to invitations. On it was written: 'Gone for ever is my strength, Old and weak am I'.

Haydn remained nominally in charge of the music at Eisenstadt until 1804 and although he had taken some part in the musical arrangements there, most of the work after 1800 had been supervised by Johann Fuchs. In 1804 Haydn formally resigned

Haydn's visiting card

* The box was severely damaged in the destruction of the Vienna City Museum during the liberation of 1945.

133

his post to Prince Esterházy. When his brother Michael declined to take over the position of *Kapellmeister* at Eisenstadt, Johann Nepomuk Hummel, the pianist and composer and sometime pupil of Mozart, was appointed.

On 31 March 1805 Haydn was unable to attend the celebrations held in honour of his seventy-third birthday. This gave rise to a report which spread through Europe that he had died. In Paris Cherubini composed a memorial cantata, and a performance of Mozart's *Requiem* was prepared as a tribute to the supposedly deceased composer. Haydn was used to hearing the news of his own death and sardonically said that he was sorry he could not travel to Paris to conduct both works.

During these last years, Haydn was frequently visited by leading musicians and personal friends, including the Abbe Vogler, the Weber family and Mozart's widow. In 1805, Ignaz Pleyel, his pupil and London rival and now a publisher, came from Paris to present a complete edition of Haydn's quartets to the composer. Pleyel's son described the visit in a letter:

Vienna, the old University. Coloured engraving by Schütz, 1790

The performance of
Haydn's *Creation*, 27
March 1808. Painting
by Wigand (Vienna,
Nationalbibliothek)

We found Haydn very feeble; he can hardly walk and after he has
spoken for a while he loses his breath. He is only seventy-three years
old, but looks as if he were eighty. He constantly says that his end is
near, that he is very old and now quite useless in the world.

Cherubini also travelled from Paris especially to see the old
man. Even Princess Esterházy came to Haydn's house to visit him
on several occasions.

Two events which provided great sorrow for the composer were
the deaths of his beloved brothers, Johann Evangelist on 10 May
1805, and Michael in August 1806. Tomasini, the violinist at
Esterháza, died on 25 April 1808 after fifty-one years in the
service of the Esterházy family.

The final triumph for Haydn was the performance in honour
of his seventy-sixth birthday of *The Creation* on 27 March 1808, in
the Great Hall of Vienna University. Although his health was
poor, the composer expressed a wish to attend the concert.
Prince Esterházy provided a carriage and, accompanied by his
doctor, Haydn set out for his last appearance in public. Outside
the hall he was cheered by a large throng of well-wishers who

135

shouted 'Long live Haydn', and trumpets and drums heralded his
entry into the building. Prince Esterházy helped him into the
hall. He was carried in a chair to a place of honour beside Princess
Esterházy. Every musician of note in the city was present, including Hummel and Salieri. The occasion proved too much for the
old man, so that it was decided that he should be taken home at
the interval. On his tearful departure, Beethoven stepped forward
to kiss his hand.

Napoleon as Emperor

Vienna, the city walls
at the Burgbastei after
French bombardment.
Gouache by Franz
Jaschke, 1809

By the beginning of 1809, Haydn was almost a complete
invalid. His last days were far from peaceful as Napoleon's
troops had invaded Vienna in the first week of May. During the
French bombardment, a cannon ball landed close to Haydn's
house, shaking the building and creating panic among the
servants. Haydn must have suffered greatly from the noise of the
guns which continued firing for over twenty-four hours.

When Vienna surrendered to the French, Napoleon ordered a
guard to be placed outside Haydn's home so that the dying man
could be protected from further discomfort. It is said that almost
every day in spite of his infirmity, Haydn played the Austrian
national anthem on his piano as an act of defiance against the
occupying forces.

In the early hours of 31 May, Haydn peacefully went into a
coma and died. In a city controlled by enemy soldiers, the news
of Haydn's death took many days to spread, and his funeral took
place almost unnoticed. On 15 June, a memorial service was held
for the composer at which appropriately Mozart's *Requiem* was

performed. Amongst the congregation were many high-ranking French officers. At first Haydn's body was buried in a Vienna cemetery, but in 1820 his remains were transferred to Eisenstadt. When the grave was opened, it was discovered that the composer's skull was missing. Two of Haydn's friends had bribed the grave-digger at the funeral to remove the head. From 1895 to 1954, the skull rested in the museum of the Gesellschaft der Musikfreunde in Vienna. Then in 1954 it was finally placed with the rest of his body in the grounds of the Bergkirche at Eisenstadt.

'A harmonious song was all my life'—Gellert, *Der Greis* (Haydn, 1799)

Index   Illustrations are indicated in **bold** type

'Heaven endowed him with genius—he is one of the immortals': Haydn, from a lead bust by his friend, Anton Grassi (E. F. Schmid)